DAILY STOICISM WITH MARCUS AURELIUS'S PHILOSOPHY

Practical Guide to the Art of Living to Achieve Inner Peace, Happiness, Confidence, Emotional Resilience, and a Stress-Free Life

JOHN HOLIDAY

Table of Contents

INTRODUCTION

Stoicism is an ancient Greek way of thinking that was developed by Zeno of Citium around 300 BC. It focuses on cultivating self-control and resilience to overcome negative emotions. The goal is not to eliminate emotions entirely but to transform them through a kind of self-discipline, marked by voluntary restraint from worldly pleasures. This practice helps individuals develop clear judgment, inner peace, and freedom from unnecessary suffering, which Stoics consider a primary objective.

Stoicism is more than just a set of ethical beliefs; it's a way of life that involves continuous practice and training. The philosophy aims to incorporate logical reasoning, Socratic dialogue, personal reflection, contemplation of death, and some form of meditation to stay present in the moment.

The term "stoic" originates from the "stoa poikile," which means "painted veranda" or "colonnade," where Zeno taught in Citium. In modern language, being stoic refers to someone who remains composed and undisturbed by emotions such as pain, pleasure, sorrow, or joy. However, this contemporary usage has drifted away from its philosophical roots.

Stoic Ethics

Stoicism, as a moral philosophy, aims for freedom from intense emotions (in the ancient sense of "fear" or "suffering") by seeking reason and "Apatheia" (an old term for apathy, implying a calm, objective, and clear judgment). It encourages indifference and a "passive" response to external events, believing that nothing outside can be inherently good or bad. Patience during life's ups and downs is also emphasized.

According to Stoics, cultivating a clear, impartial, and disciplined mindset enables one to understand "logos" – the universal natural reason present in all things. They argue that misfortune and wrongdoing result from ignorance, and the solution lies in practicing Stoic philosophy. This involves examining one's judgments and behavior to align them with the universal foundation of nature. Hence, the well-known Stoic maxim: "Living according to nature," meaning living in harmony with both the laws of the universe and human reason.

Stoicism shares some similarities with Siddhartha Gautama's teachings in Buddhism, particularly the Four Noble Truths:

1) Life involves suffering;
2) Suffering stems from desire and attachment;
3) Freedom from suffering comes from letting go of desires;
4) Moral moderation and self-discipline lead to liberation.

A key aspect of Stoicism is to enhance individuals' ethical and moral well-being by aligning their will with nature and practicing the four cardinal virtues (derived from Plato): wisdom ("Sophia"), courage ("Andreia"), justice ("dikaiosyne"), and moderation ("sophrosyne").

Stoics believe that living in accordance with reason and ideals means living in harmony with the fundamental order of the universe. They advocate for equality among individuals, challenging societal norms such as slavery and emphasizing that all are "children of God." They reject external distinctions like social rank and wealth in determining social relationships.

While Stoicism acknowledges determinism to some extent, stating that we act according to the world's needs, it emphasizes conscious acceptance of obedience to the law. The Roman philosopher Seneca the Younger, a prominent Stoic, delved into the philosophical aspects of anger. He viewed anger as a rational problem that could be addressed through logical arguments, not just an uncontrollable emotional outburst. Seneca advocated for a more realistic and pessimistic attitude to avoid excessive expectations and subsequent anger.

Other Principles

In Stoic philosophy, there are additional principles related to logic and epistemology. They emphasize the certainty of knowledge, achievable through reason and by carefully considering personal experiences and the collective judgment of humanity. According to Stoics, our senses regularly receive sensations, like pulses, from objects, which leave impressions on the mind. The mind can then either approve or reject these impressions to distinguish between reality and false images. This stands in contrast to Plato's idealism, where knowledge comes only from the mind, and the senses are seen as sources of illusions and errors.

Unlike those with religious beliefs, Stoic students acknowledge a material world governed by rational principles, often referred to as God or nature. This world is divided into passive elements (like critical matter) and active elements (such as fate or guiding principles). Examples of active elements include intelligence, primitive fire, or an instrument that acts upon passive matter.

Human and animal spirits are seen as manifestations of this primitive fire and are subject to destiny. The philosopher Heraclitus, influential to Stoicism, proposed the idea that everything is fire, envisioning a cyclical history where the world burns and then returns.

For Stoics, everything is considered material, and there is no realm beyond materialism. Even words and God Himself are viewed as material. Emotions are seen as substantial because they have physical manifestations, like blushing or smiling. The mind or soul is reduced to matter because the body triggers thoughts or sensations in the soul, and the soul, in turn, prompts movements in the body – a connection made possible by sharing the same substance.

Stoics also held the belief in the unity of the entire world (monism) and the idea that a divine reality permeates everything (pantheism). They saw the universe as a vast living body, with central parts like the stars or the sun. All components are interconnected, meaning events in one place can influence what happens in another. According to Stoicism, everything in the world is predetermined, or destined, although humans possess a specific free will, akin to vortices playing a role in the flow of all rivers.

CHAPTER 1: WHAT IS STOICISM?

The term "stoic" today suggests being indifferent to all emotions, whether intense love or strong hatred, but the actual philosophy of stoicism goes beyond this common understanding.

Stoicism originated with a Greek philosopher in Athens named Zeno of Citium, though some of the most well-known Stoic thinkers include Seneca the Younger and Marcus Aurelius, who was a Stoic emperor in Rome.

At its core, stoicism asserts that negative emotions arise from poor judgment, and its main goal is to conquer these destructive forces through self-control. The Stoics advocate for achieving genuine success through inner strength, presenting philosophy as a way of life that leads to wisdom.

A wise person, according to Stoicism, has attained ethical and intellectual perfection. Happiness, they argue, is rooted in virtue, making a wise individual resilient against misfortune because virtue is not influenced by luck. This philosophy empowers individuals to feel in control of their destiny.

Stoicism also delves into the concepts of human destiny and free will. While Stoics embrace determinism, the belief that past events shape all future occurrences (akin to fate), they also uphold the idea of individual free will. This combination leads to both an acceptance of what will be and an effort to shape a better future.

Control is a key virtue in Stoicism. They stress the importance of being in control of oneself, comparing a person without control to a dog tied to a cart, following wherever it goes. On the other hand, a stoic or virtuous person is depicted as someone who chooses their own path. Stoic virtues are not based on religious ethics but are viewed as naturalistic ethics – being a good person is valuable for its own sake, even without consideration of an afterlife.

Logic is another fundamental aspect of Stoicism. They assert that knowledge can only be acquired through logic and truth, emphasizing the importance of understanding natural phenomena without resorting to superstitions.

"Tell yourself early in the morning: I will meet ungrateful, violent, insidious, jealous, implacable men today. All these things have come across ignorance of good and evil ... I cannot hurt them because nobody becomes wrong, nor can I be angry with my relatives or hate them because we were born to work together." - Marcus Aurelius

History of Stoicism

The story of Stoicism begins in Athens around 300 BC when Zeno of Citium introduced the philosophy. Zeno, a student of Thebes' major thinkers, adapted behavioral theories and incorporated more practical and moderate aspects. In its early stages, Stoicism challenged superstitions and taboos, asserting that the moral law aligns with nature.

Cleanthes of Assos succeeded Zeno, and his influential student, Chrysippus of Soli, played a pivotal role in shaping Stoicism (around 280-207 BC). Chrysippus unified the philosophy, combining formal logic, materialistic physics, and naturalistic ethics. While ethics remained the primary focus, Stoicism's logical theories gained attention from later philosophers.

Stoicism flourished as the most significant school in the Greco-Roman world, particularly among educated elites. It produced notable figures like Panaetius of Rhodes, Posidonius, Cato the Younger, Seneca the Younger, Epictetus, and Marcus Aurelius.

Later on, a movement known as Neo-Stoicism emerged, blending Stoicism with Christianity. Founded by the Belgian humanist Justus Lipsius (1547-1606), Neo-Stoicism is a practical philosophy emphasizing that living righteously involves resisting passions (such as greed, joy, fear, and sadness) and submitting to a higher power, namely God.

Stoicism, an ancient philosophical school, was established around 301 BC by Zeno of Citium, a Phoenician merchant, in Athens. Originally named Zenonism, it became known as Stoicism because Zeno and his followers conducted their meetings in the Stoa Poikile or painted Portico.

Unlike other philosophical schools, Stoicism was unique in that its practitioners, known as stoics, engaged in debates openly on porches where anyone could listen. This accessibility earned it the reputation of being a "street philosophy," catering not only to aristocrats but also to ordinary people.

For nearly five centuries, Stoicism flourished as one of the most influential and respected schools of philosophy. It was embraced by people from all walks of life, be they rich or poor, powerful or suffering, all in pursuit of the good life. However, over the course of almost two millennia, this once essential knowledge faded into obscurity.

The revival of Stoicism began in the 1970s, particularly fueled by its incorporation into Cognitive Behavioral Therapy (CBT) and the writings of authors like William Irvine and Ryan Holiday.

The question arises: How did the wisdom of Stoicism survive the centuries of obscurity?

Contrary to expectations, ancient documents from stoic teachers and practitioners were preserved. Three key figures played a crucial role in preserving Stoic teachings:

Marcus Aurelius: The last sensible emperor of the Roman Empire, Marcus Aurelius, wrote a private diary reflecting on each day, which was later published as a book on meditation. This diary serves as a significant source of Stoic philosophy.

Epictetus: Born a slave, Epictetus became a legendary figure, founding his school and teaching influential Roman thinkers, including Marcus Aurelius. His teachings were transcribed by his student, Arrian, in works like "Discourses" and "Enchiridion."

Seneca: Tutor and advisor to Emperor Nero, Seneca was not only a wise ruler but also a renowned playwright. Despite his tragic fate, as Nero forced him to commit suicide, many of Seneca's personal letters have survived, providing valuable insights into Stoic philosophy.

These documents from the main Stoic leaders form the foundation of our understanding of Stoicism, allowing this ancient wisdom to endure and find relevance in the modern world.

The Most Influential Stoic Philosophers

Imagine yourself amidst the bustling crowd at the Circus Maximus, the air filled with fervent cheers as chariots race by and gladiators engage in fierce combat. Amidst this chaos, our main characters, the Stoic philosophers, imparted their wisdom. While the excitement of the Colosseum may seem more gripping, it is Stoic philosophy that has endured through the ages.

In the following chapters, we'll delve into the lives and teachings of three prominent Roman Stoics whose writings have stood the test of time: Seneca, Epictetus, and Marcus Aurelius. Although countless books on Stoicism have been lost to history, the works of these luminaries remain, forming the bedrock of Stoic thought.

Despite their flaws, these remarkable individuals were deeply engaged in society, striving to improve the world around them. Among them, we encounter a wealthy playwright akin to a modern-day entrepreneur, an early advocate for women's rights, and a disabled former slave who would profoundly influence the most powerful person in the world, the Roman Emperor. While we can only scratch the surface of their fascinating lives in this book, their contributions to Stoic philosophy are profound and enduring.

Marcus Aurelius: The Stoic Emperor

Marcus Aurelius stands as the final among five commendable Roman emperors and is considered one of the greatest Stoic philosophers in history. He embodies Plato's vision of an ideal philosopher king. But how did his life unfold to make him one of Rome's most exceptional rulers?

Born in Rome, Marcus faced adversity early on, losing his father when he was just three years old. Despite the challenges, the lessons from his father's few memories and stories instilled humility and a strong sense of duty in him. Following his father's death, he was adopted by his grandfather on his father's side.

At a tender age of six, Marcus joined a religious order named the Knights, at the behest of Emperor Hadrian. Although the order was traditionally for older children, Marcus excelled, impressing Hadrian with his dedication and quickly rising in ranks.

Despite marrying Hadrian's stepdaughter, Commodus, and entering a political role, Marcus found himself often alone due to Hadrian's extended absences from Rome. It was during this time that he encountered the teachings of stoicism through a philosopher named Apollonius, who left a profound impact on him.

Upon Hadrian's death, Antoninus Pius became the new emperor and, in an unexpected turn, requested Marcus to be his heir. Initially taken aback, Marcus moved from his mother's house to Hadrian's private residence. Antoninus sought to maintain continuity in government, and he admired Marcus for his virtue and dignity.

During his time in power, Marcus faced personal tragedies, losing at least four children, a pain he eloquently expressed in his writings. Despite the challenges, Marcus remained committed to his stoic philosophy, striving to balance his responsibilities as emperor while staying true to his principles.

Marcus reluctantly accepted Pius's request to live in the Imperial Palace and remarried Faustina, his sister-in-law, as advised by Pius for political consolidation. Although not a romantic union, the marriage resulted in several children.

Throughout his rule, Marcus Aurelius demonstrated a unique blend of stoic wisdom and imperial responsibilities, leaving an enduring legacy as both a capable ruler and a philosopher who grappled with the complexities of life.

Seneca the Younger

Lucius Annaeus Seneca, often referred to as Seneca the Younger or simply Seneca, was a controversial figure in Stoic philosophy. He was born in Cordoba, Spain, around the time of Jesus, and received his education in Rome, Italy. Seneca is widely recognized as one of the greatest writers of ancient times, and many of his essays and personal letters have survived, providing valuable insights into Stoic philosophy. What makes his writings resonate with us is his focus on practical aspects of Stoicism, covering topics ranging from everyday life advice to handling intense emotions like grief or anger.

Seneca led a remarkable life that invites scrutiny. Aside from his enduring letters, he gained fame as a successful playwright and amassed considerable wealth through astute financial ventures, akin to a modern entrepreneur or investor. However, his life wasn't without controversy. He was exiled to Corsica for having an affair with the emperor's niece, only to be recalled to Rome later to tutor Nero, the emperor's son.

Under Nero's reign, Seneca rose to prominence as an advisor and became one of the wealthiest individuals in the Roman Empire. Despite espousing Stoic principles, his immense wealth sometimes led to accusations of hypocrisy. Moreover, his association with Nero, a notorious and tyrannical ruler, raises further questions about his character. In 65 CE, Nero compelled Seneca to take his own life on suspicions of treason.

Despite the complexities of his life, Seneca's commitment to Stoicism remained steadfast. He grappled with his imperfections through philosophy and introspection. His letters, filled with wisdom and inspiration, continue to be studied and quoted extensively, serving as a timeless guide for understanding Stoic principles.

Epictetus

Epictetus, a significant figure in Stoic philosophy, had a humble beginning as a slave in Hierapolis, which is now known as Pamukkale in Turkey. His original name is lost to history, as "Epictetus" simply means "property" or "something that was bought." He was owned by Epaphroditos, a wealthy freedman who served as a secretary to Emperor Nero in Rome. Despite being crippled in one leg, whether from birth or due to an injury, Epictetus received a fortunate opportunity to study Stoic philosophy under the guidance of the esteemed teacher Musonius Rufus, courtesy of his kind master Epaphroditos.

Following Nero's demise in 68 CE, Epictetus was emancipated, a common practice for educated slaves in Rome. He established his own school and taught Stoic principles for nearly twenty-five years until Emperor Domitian's decree banished philosophers from

Rome. Epictetus relocated his school to Nicopolis, Greece, leading a modest life with minimal possessions. Despite the upheavals, Stoicism regained popularity after Domitian's assassination, and Epictetus emerged as its foremost teacher. Although he could have returned to Rome, he chose to remain in Nicopolis until his passing around 135 CE.

Epictetus's school, although situated in Nicopolis, attracted students from across the Roman Empire. He imparted teachings on maintaining dignity and tranquility amidst life's challenges, a hallmark of Stoic philosophy.

Similar to his mentor Musonius Rufus, Epictetus did not write any texts himself. However, his lectures were meticulously recorded by his devoted student Arrian, resulting in the famous Discourses. Arrian also compiled the Enchiridion, a concise summary of Epictetus's key principles. The Enchiridion, often translated as "Handbook," serves as a practical guide, readily accessible for confronting life's adversities, akin to a trusty dagger always at hand.

Stoicism in the Face of Adversity

In late 2011, Thailand faced major floods due to unprecedented rainfall in the northern region, covering an area larger than Belgium. Floodwaters reached five meters in some areas, affecting millions of people. Despite challenging conditions, the local population, particularly in Bangkok, mobilized to help those in need. Ayutthaya, the old capital, faced prolonged flooding, but people understood the need to save Bangkok to prevent catastrophic long-term effects.

The disaster claimed 800 lives, directly affecting around 13 million people. Remarkably, there were no reports of looting, and people assisted each other. This stoic response differed significantly from the post-Katrina scenes in New Orleans. The resilience and selflessness shown in Asia during crises are not new; similar stoic responses were witnessed during the 2004 tsunami that affected Indonesia, India, Thailand, and Sri Lanka.

In southern Thailand, the island of Phi Phi was entirely devastated, but reconstruction efforts began promptly. Communities, despite their shock and pain, came together for the greater good. Similarly, Japan faced immense challenges with the 2011 earthquake and tsunami, resulting in a remarkable show of resilience. Despite a high death toll, the response demonstrated the strength and character of the Japanese people, even in the face of a 45-meter-high tsunami and the meltdown of Fukushima's nuclear reactors.

Throughout these challenges, the people of Asia consistently displayed pride, dignity, and a sense of collective responsibility. The world could draw valuable lessons from their stoic responses to adversity.

CHAPTER 2: STOICISM AND PSYCHOLOGY

Can Stoicism Improve Your Life? Connection Between Stoicism and Positive Psychology

S toicism isn't just a theory; it's a set of practices meant to enhance our lives. The big question is whether these Stoic practices actually work and make people's lives better. To answer this, we turn to psychology and its scientific methods. In this chapter, I delve into the efforts of the Stoicism Today team, who are using psychology to address the question, "Can Stoicism make a positive impact?" I also suggest directions for future research. About fifteen years ago, a new branch of psychology emerged, focusing on understanding what contributes to a good life and how to enhance it.

Positive Psychology

Positive psychology, established in 1998, has conducted various experiments, written many books, and delivered lectures. While philosophers and self-help authors have traditionally explored what we ought to do, positive psychology goes a step further by suggesting planned activities (called "interventions") and scientifically testing their impact. One method involves asking people to try these interventions and measuring their well-being before and after to observe any changes.

Positive psychology has yielded significant findings. For instance, positive emotions like happiness, pride, love, and even fear, when experienced in a functional way, can have positive consequences, such as improved health, creativity, and altruism.

"Flow" is crucial for well-being, where you fully concentrate on what you're doing. Unlike pleasure, flow is an immersive experience where you don't necessarily feel anything during the activity.

Maintaining positive attitudes, including hope, optimism, gratitude, and a belief in personal growth, has been proven to contribute to better health, improved work and study performance, higher self-esteem, and enhanced resilience.

Identified positive behaviors include recognizing and using one's strengths and engaging in acts of kindness. Simple measures have been shown to boost well-being both in the short term and over six months. Interestingly, some interventions that seem reasonable may not result in lasting positive changes.

Now, there's solid evidence that reading good science and applying that knowledge to oneself, groups, and education can lead to increased well-being.

Philosophy and Positive Psychology

While the progress in positive psychology is great, there are some important questions from a philosophical perspective that it should consider, such as:

- What does it really mean to have well-being, and how does it differ from related terms like subjective well-being, prosperity, pleasure, enjoyment, and happiness?

- Positive psychology emphasizes both feeling good and doing good. Where does virtue fit into the picture? How important is it to be an excellent person?
- Can positive attitudes and behavior be harmful if displayed by someone lacking virtue? For instance, should we be concerned if a person with harmful intentions uses their strengths?
- Wisdom, a virtue valued by many ancient philosophers, is it especially important? Is it not just about being confident and optimistic, but also about using these qualities wisely?
- Can the practical ideas put forth by philosophers, including Stoics and thinkers, be put to the test?
- Could philosophies that have been empirically tested help individuals become virtuous and wise, feel better, and ultimately strengthen the field of positive psychology?

Putting Stoicism to the Test: Stoicism Today and Practical Exercises

Stoicism is a great fit for examination in critical psychology, thanks to its powerful therapeutic purpose and the abundance of practical ideas found in the writings of Marcus Aurelius, Seneca, and especially Epictetus. Led by a university professor, the Stoicism Today group, in collaboration with the author, initiated the testing of Stoicism.

In a study conducted in 2013, participants, both from the general public and those familiar with Stoicism, were provided with a free eBook containing Stoic readings and reflective exercises, some of which were available as audio recordings. Additionally, a blog was maintained, and participants formed the core of primary education, engaging with each other through social networks. The study incorporated daily meditations and exercises for "Stoic Week," featuring specific themes and morning and evening reflections combined with various Stoic ideas.

Recommended Activities for Practicing Stoicism:

- Morning Meditation: Focus on a stoic principle, like "concentrating only on things within our control" or "approaching potential challenges stoically" to set a positive tone for the day.
- Late-Night Reflection: Evaluate how you handled challenges throughout the day using stoic principles. Acknowledge what you did well and make a commitment to do even better the next day.
- Daily Exercises: Engage in daily exercises covering topics such as understanding what is within our control, practicing stoic self-discipline and flexibility, incorporating stoic phrases from a database, gaining stoic insights, managing emotions and challenges, and fostering philanthropy and resilience.
- Stoic Check Sheet: Utilize a stoic check sheet to enhance awareness of what is within your control and what is not.

As part of Stoic Week, participants were requested to complete various questionnaires before and after the program to assess changes in their well-being and the extent to which they embraced stoic principles.

Evidence of Stoicism's Impact: Results and Insights

The outcomes from our study provide strong support for the effectiveness of Stoicism; it has passed its initial examination. Members experienced a 14% boost in life fulfillment, a 9% increase in positive feelings, and an 11% decrease in negative feelings.

These findings indicate that practicing Stoicism has a meaningful positive influence, addressing some common criticisms. For instance, optimism saw an impressive 18% increase. Moreover, the study affirmed some positive expectations for Stoicism; it seems to enhance satisfaction and reduce anger.

Additionally, the results suggest that Stoicism not only contributes to well-being but also promotes virtue. A significant majority (56%) of participants reported feeling 80% or more that Stoicism made them better individuals and wiser.

The Stoicism Today project aimed not only to measure changes in well-being but also to explore the connection between well-being and Stoic attitudes and behaviors. For this purpose, a scale called the Stoic Attitudes and Behaviors Scales (SABS) was developed and tested, offering valuable insights into how Stoicism relates to overall well-being. The study revealed that certain non-Stoic behaviors, such as prioritizing pleasure and comfort over doing what is right, had a negative impact on well-being.

Key Aspects of Stoicism That Bring the Most Benefits:

Stoic Awareness: This involves consistently being mindful of the nature of our judgments and actions. It's about paying close attention to how we think and behave.

Stoic Commitment to Thoughts: It's about recognizing that troubling thoughts are just impressions in our minds and don't necessarily represent the reality of a situation. This helps in managing our reactions to challenging thoughts.

Affinity for Others: This means viewing ourselves as an integral part of the human race, similar to how a limb is a part of the human body. It encourages a sense of connection and shared humanity.

Stoic Pre-Meditation: This involves the practice of foreseeing potential future challenges and mentally preparing for them in a systematic manner, considering various scenarios in an orderly fashion.

Exploring Future Avenues

While the current findings are promising, it's crucial to conduct further research that meets strict scientific standards. Here are some priorities for future exploration:

Rigorous Controlled Experiments: Conduct more robust experiments with careful controls. Follow-up assessments, such as after 3 or 6 months, and the inclusion of control groups would enhance the reliability of the results.

Enhancement of Stoic Attitudes and Behavior Scale (SABS): The SABS scale, a tool measuring adherence to Stoicism and its link to well-being, shows promise. It could benefit from refinement, including simplifying the language used and incorporating feedback from individuals who identify as Stoics.

Long-Term Analysis of SABS Results: While SABS results show correlations between well-being and Stoicism, they don't confirm that adopting Stoic practices leads to changes in well-being. To address this, longitudinal studies could track participants who specifically engage in Stoic attitudes and behaviors, providing clearer insights.

Improvement of Materials and Programs: Similar to mindfulness programs derived from Buddhist practices, there's potential to refine stoically inspired programs. These could be tailored for specific challenges, like anger management or addressing long-term health conditions such as diabetes and coronary heart disease, offering targeted support based on Stoic principles.

Stoicism in the Context of Positive Psychology

Although more research is needed, I believe we've gathered enough evidence to support the inclusion of Stoic exercises in evidence-based wellness practices. In this final section, I want to emphasize that Stoicism holds a unique value in helping positive psychology promote virtue and wisdom, enabling individuals to both feel and do good.

Positive psychologists have explored virtues in literature and identified six virtues, incorporating the four main virtues from ancient Greece: wisdom, courage, self-control, and justice. While Stoics and other ancient thinkers believed all these virtues were essential for a good life, positive psychologists encourage people to recognize and utilize their strengths, which are more specific and practical expressions of virtues. For instance, the virtue of wisdom is broken down into strengths like creativity, curiosity, judgment, love of learning, and perspective. There's solid evidence that leveraging one's strengths enhances well-being.

However, the approach of positive psychologists focuses on identifying and using existing strengths. It remains uncertain whether this approach is the most effective way to cultivate virtue. Some argue that true virtue might require acknowledging and working on the moral traits one lacks. For example, if someone is brave but lacks self-control, should they emphasize bravery or work on developing self-control? Socrates suggests in Pools that, depending on the circumstances, withdrawal may be more effective than confrontation.

Stoicism encourages individuals to focus on what they can control and consider the well-being of others. This approach aids in skill development, offering a positive education where individuals can refine their practices and make progress.

Do Stoics Experience Less Anger Compared to Others?

Previous reports from Stoic Week have consistently highlighted the positive connection between stability and peace. In Stoic Week 2019, the analysis of the initial questionnaire explored whether this relationship persisted. The research delves into the link between stoicism and anger, assessed through the anger disorder scale (ADS-S). Additionally, a new version of the Stoic Attitudes and Behaviours scale (SABS v5.0) was introduced, highlighting which chapters from the scale are most and least connected to life satisfaction, personal growth, positive and negative emotions, and anger. Essentially, this report pinpoints which aspects of stoicism appear to have the most significant impact on these outcomes. Other parts of this series discuss the effects of participating in Stoic Week (part 3), summarize participant feedback, and propose future research directions (part 4). For further details on the methods used, refer to the appendices in this report.

How Does My Score Compare to Others?

If you took part in Stoic Week, you received averages of certain measures for participants at the beginning of a past Stoic Week. However, at that time, we didn't have data for the 2019 Stoic Week, including comparative values for the anger scale or the new SABS scale. Now, I have the details. Let's look at the average scores:

- Life Satisfaction (SWL): 23
- Emotions (SPANE): 5

- Thrive: 43
- Anger (ADS-S): 34
- Stoicism (SABS 5.0): 300

The new SABS scale, introduced in Stoic Week 2019, is a 60-point questionnaire (explained in Appendix A). This scale has been refined based on previous work, eliminating items with lower psychometric properties. We are currently working on validating SABS 5.0 and developing subscales like "Stoic Worldview" and "Values Awareness and Stoic Mindfulness." As this work on subscales is still in the early stages, details will be shared later.

Stoicism and Dealing with Anger

In theory, we expect that practicing stoicism can be helpful in handling anger. The idea is that people who follow stoic principles are not only expected to experience less anger but are also less likely to become angry compared to those who don't follow stoicism. This is because non-stoics often get angry about things that are beyond their control.

Previous research from Stoic Week hinted at a strong connection between stoicism and reduced anger, but it was based on a single question about anger in the SPANE questionnaire. Since effectively managing anger can be a significant benefit of stoicism, we felt the need to explore this relationship further. In our recent study, participants were asked to complete a validated anger questionnaire called the 18-point ADS-S questionnaire. This allowed us to understand the link between stoicism and anger more thoroughly, considering various aspects such as the intensity of anger, the tendency to seek revenge, and observable angry behavior.

CHAPTER 3: STOICISM AND EMOTIONS

People often mistakenly believe that a stoic, someone who follows stoic philosophy, is emotionless and lacks feelings, whether positive ones like happiness and love or negative ones like anger and fear. However, this is a misunderstanding. To grasp why this perception exists, it's crucial to understand how stoics view emotions.

The key concept to consider is the stoic's indifference. Let me break it down for you. A stoic doesn't attach value or significance to many things that society deems important. For instance, imagine a stranger staring at you. While some non-stoics might feel bothered by it, a stoic doesn't see the importance of this action when observed objectively.

Similarly, stoics don't place importance on wealth or poverty. This might be a bit tricky to comprehend, so let me clarify. Stoics believe that true happiness is achieved through virtue, aligning with nature. According to this belief, external circumstances, such as wealth or poverty, don't determine one's happiness. Even if you face challenges, as long as you act virtuously and find happiness within, external factors become less significant.

It's important to note that stoics aren't indifferent to the well-being of others; many wealthy individuals who follow stoicism use their resources to help people.

Stoics view negative emotions as irrational feelings that wrongly convince us of the importance of certain things. To illustrate, let's examine four basic negative emotions: fear, desire, lust, and joy. Fear arises from the worry of not obtaining something we deem essential. Desire and joy result from getting what we want, even if it's not truly beneficial. Stoics aim to recognize and overcome these illogical feelings to attain a more tranquil and meaningful life.

Stoicism: A World Governed by Reason, Stripped of Emotion

Stoicism, a philosophy that aimed to enhance the Roman Empire, was widely believed in ancient Rome, in recent decades, and is still embraced by many today. The core idea was for individuals to live with controlled emotions and rely on reason to make decisions. If the principles of stoicism had been precisely adopted, it could have saved the Roman Empire from its downfall. However, when we objectively reflect on these principles without emotions, we uncover the ironic truth that a human world dominated by stoicism, guided by the philosopher king Plato, and shaped by the ideals of Marcus Aurelius, might seem inhuman.

While stoicism was the prevailing philosophy in Rome, like many idealistic concepts, it was never fully implemented by the general population. Stoicism, at its core, is a description of the universal law and common reason. To practice stoicism means not just acknowledging this fact but using that knowledge to control and conquer oneself. However, expecting an entire society to adhere to a specific moral and social order may be unrealistic. Despite this, the impracticality should not be an excuse to abandon a necessity, prompting us to delve deeper into the philosophy.

The concept of stoicism, understanding the natural law with reason to conquer passions and make impartial judgments, is intriguing yet inherently flawed in practice. Ironically, to identify the errors in stoicism, one must view it from a stoic perspective—someone already influenced by stoicism. Analyzing its principles requires using stoicism itself.

The conquest of passions and the application of common law through reason, as advocated by stoicism, contradicts our human nature. Our passions define our humanity, providing the strength and ambition to face countless adversities. The wild and uncontrolled passion of a lover, the emotional depth revealed in a poet's work, and the daring pursuit of discoveries by a sailor—all showcase the power of passion.

Stoicism fails to acknowledge that love is often irrational, and passions, while guided by reason, remain an essential part of our existence. The combination of uninhibited passion and purposeful reason leads to the balanced virtue of wisdom. Following reason alone or completely abandoning passions are both undesirable extremes.

A life governed solely by reason might be enlightening, but it would lack the vibrant spices that make life enjoyable. Stoicism's focus on "the true and the good, wisdom and virtue" is edifying but may become monotonous as it fails to capture the richness of human experience.

Stoicism, like any human teaching, has inherent imperfections. While it may lack in portraying a fully engaging and passionate lifestyle, it offers a personal perspective that doesn't fully connect with the depth of human experience, as noted by Kierkegaard. Beauty, like life, can be explained through reason, but true understanding comes from passionate engagement with activities and inner experiences.

The Impact of Stoicism on Our Lives and Others

During a conversation with a new client about their administrative needs, I inquired, "What are you doing administratively?" I took a moment to consider and then confidently responded that I could handle anything. To clarify, I suggested they share their specific needs, and I would assess if I could assist them on a case-by-case basis.

At first glance, my response might appear a bit bold, depending on how you interpret it. To reiterate, I asserted that I could handle anything, without mentioning potential challenges or occasional mistakes. This, however, is a distinct issue that may arise, and it's important to acknowledge it.

This isn't just about claiming that people can do everything. The crucial question is whether individuals have the dedication and resilience to assess the outcomes of their actions. Most importantly, it involves examining how they interpret the inevitable missteps, setbacks, and errors that are part of our human experience.

Failure is a natural part of life. Our response to these setbacks reflects our sense of justice, and our ability to navigate through challenges highlights our strengths. These factors play a pivotal role in the process of maturing and navigating life's journey.

Stoicism - Quite a Powerful Concept!

Stoicism, as per the dictionary, is described as "holding back emotions and being indifferent to pleasure or pain." Back in ancient Greece and Rome, the Stoics believed that to attain happiness and wisdom, individuals should control their emotions tightly and avoid displaying joy or sadness. Even today, many view stoicism as something admirable, especially if it aligns with a keen sense of knowledge.

Picture this: in ancient times, deep thinkers, philosophers, and even Roman figures like politicians and military strategists may have embraced stoicism as a way to set themselves apart from the masses, showcasing a perceived superiority. Fast forward to today, and stoicism remains prevalent in society, where emotions are often suppressed rather than accepted, creating a facade that hides the truth.

A wise person once said, "Truth is suffering...". This implies that exploring life's challenges and the subsequent pains is not widely supported. Many fail to understand how this attitude reflects both intangibly and physically. Without experiencing pain, one cannot truly appreciate joy—a natural ebb and flow that spans the entire spectrum of human consciousness.

Modern society often struggles to accurately gauge external appearances. Narratives that depict a person's journey from hardship to success often lean on beliefs associated with stoic attitudes, presenting a skewed version of truth.

In contrast to ancient Stoics' beliefs, wisdom isn't accumulated, and true happiness comes from honestly examining the harmful intentions hidden in interpretations. Candid self-reflection reveals this understanding to those committed to living authentically. Overcoming a Texan-sized ego is no easy feat, and it's even more challenging to undo the consequences of stoicism once it takes hold.

Stoicism doesn't allow others to witness the struggle and fall. To truly live authentically, one must question interpretations with maturity. Courage, sincerity, and authenticity stem from acknowledging unknown factors and correcting course when necessary, not from stoic suppression.

So, when faced with the challenges of stoicism, I found a deeper understanding of its nature—a beast, indeed. I responded to my client with empathy, acknowledging the power of stoicism without dismissing my own mistakes. Let's strive for a world where people don't guess or question, but recognize, appreciate, and manage fragility when necessary. It's about making small course corrections as needed, embracing the journey of life, and understanding the intricate matrix that surrounds us.

Stoicism: Are Some People Stoic in Childhood?

When it comes to personal growth, much has been said about the importance of practicing self-control and resilience. These are crucial skills to have in life. Without self-control, it becomes challenging to achieve valuable goals, and one might find themselves caught up in endless distractions.

Imagine a child in a toy store as an analogy to understand the consequences of lacking self-control. The child moves from one area to another in an instant, unable to focus on any particular toy. Similarly, as adults, if we can't control ourselves, it can affect various aspects of our lives, such as our career or health.

If individuals can't control their thoughts and feelings, it could harm their lives, making them vulnerable like a small boat in the vast ocean rather than a sturdy ship. Inability to cope with setbacks may hinder their progress, as they lack the emotional strength needed to face life's challenges.

It's akin to going to the gym but refusing to lift anything substantial. While it might make the task easier, it won't make them stronger. Enduring pain becomes crucial for personal development.

However, there's a dark side to being stoic. Taking it to the extreme might lead to denying emotions and suppressing feelings, creating an internal struggle between mind and body. While it can help achieve goals, it may hinder interpersonal connections, making individuals seem emotionally distant and lonely.

For some, adopting stoicism may stem from a troubled relationship with emotions or a belief that being stoic requires denying feelings. This denial might be a defense mechanism to avoid facing internal wounds, often rooted in early childhood experiences where emotional needs weren't met.

Those who had to endure extreme pain and suppress emotions during early childhood may naturally be drawn to stoicism. However, this form of stoicism could serve as another defense mechanism to avoid confronting internal injuries. Seeking external support, such as therapy or guidance from a healer, becomes essential for those who want to integrate their emotions and become more complete individuals.

CHAPTER 4: STEPS TOWARDS PRACTICAL STOICISM

#1 Practical Stoicism: Simply Living

Isn't it crazy and downright foolish to desire so much when we can only hold so little? - Seneca

It's madness to believe that the quantity of money matters more than one's state of mind. Personally, I'd choose dealing with illness over indulging in luxury. Why? Because illness harms only the body, while luxury harms both the body and the soul. Luxury leads to physical weakness, cowardice, and a lack of self-control. It also breeds injustice and greed, causing a failure in duties towards friends, the city, and the gods. To avoid injustice, we must steer clear of luxury and extravagance in every aspect.

It might seem natural to desire the finer things in life, like a bigger house, a fancier car, or a more exotic vacation. Who wouldn't want those? But let's not worry too much about it. Our life's purpose isn't to consume the best of everything. Instead, it's about achieving "realization" through developing an exceptional character.

Chasing after luxury interferes with the pursuit of virtue; you can't focus on both. Indulging in luxury creates a mental link with temporary, external things that are beyond our control. It sets us on a dangerous path of constantly wanting more, becoming slaves to our desires.

The "good life" is quite the opposite. The material possessions and intense sensations that many see as markers of success are, in fact, self-imposed obstacles. The wise person aims to eliminate anything from their life that doesn't contribute to their goals because distractions are, at best, hindrances.

Perfection isn't achieved by adding more but by removing what's unnecessary, as Antoine de Saint-Exupry wisely said. The things of real value reside within you—your sense of justice, your self-discipline. Everything else is just noise and baggage.

#2 *Practical Stoicism: Use Your Head*

I find contentment when my actions align with nature—what I aim to achieve and avoid. Following nature means acting intentionally, purposefully, and with consent, not necessarily hugging trees or dancing with satyrs, but behaving in ways that lead to personal flourishing. These principles are effective and creative, supported by the laws of society, and ignoring them brings unfortunate consequences.

To practice stoicism effectively, one needs a solid understanding of philosophy, particularly the branch that deals with the fundamental nature of things—physics. Ancient physics encompassed cosmological, scientific, and comparative aspects, helping us understand the nature of reality.

Following nature involves recognizing the facts about the physical and social world, understanding our strengths, relationships, goals, motivations, thoughts, emotions, and expectations. It emphasizes critical thinking about authority and encourages using reason to examine facts and determine the right course of action.

Understanding this process reveals that all other stoic teachings are derived from the primary rule: follow nature. When unsure about what's right, facing conflicting maxims, or when the rules aren't intuitive, the answer is to return to the source and follow nature. In simpler terms, it means "use your head." Adapt to changing facts, seek more information when needed, and change direction if your current path doesn't make sense. The key is to use what works and take it where you find it.

In a living philosophy like stoicism, there's no rigid orthodoxy. Making it work for you is what matters, and you can't go wrong if you apply these principles effectively.

#3 Practical Stoicism: Amor Fati

Instead of wishing things to happen as you want them to, ask for the strength to handle them the way you want, and you'll do well. Shape your will and draw others along with it.

My guiding principle for what's admirable in humanity is love, but not just enduring the unavoidable or pretending it doesn't exist. Love it all—what's behind, before, and for eternity. It's not about merely putting up with the inevitable; it's about genuinely loving it.

When philosophers speak of Amor Fati, or "love your fate," they're referring to embracing even the challenging aspects of life. Loving your fate is easy when you've just won the lottery, but the true challenge is to love it even when it's tough. It might seem stoic to just smile and endure, but that's not sufficient.

The key is to understand that fate, with all its challenges, makes us stronger. A life without challenges would make us weak and lead to dull and ordinary existence. Our daily struggles build our resilience and backbone. When we face attacks, job losses, insults, or thefts, we have the chance to respond with virtue, gaining resilience, strength, and wisdom.

How we respond to our fate shapes our character. Our interactions with challenges determine who we become. To be truly great, to earn respect, we need formidable challenges to reject and overcome. This is why we learn to genuinely love our destiny — not just endure it — because it makes us better. Without these challenges, who would we be?

#4 Practical Stoicism: Enjoy The Silence

Avoid talking about people, be it in terms of praise, guilt, or confrontation. - Epictetus

Prioritize silence as your usual approach. Speak only when necessary and get straight to the point. However, if the situation demands it, engage in conversation sparingly, avoiding general topics like gladiators, horse racing, athletes, and endless discussions about food and drink.

If there's an awkward pause in conversation, embrace it. If you're not enjoying a conversation, it's okay to stay silent. There's nothing wrong with allowing moments of quiet.

It's essential to note that maintaining complete silence, like monks do, isn't suitable in social settings where participation is expected. Answer questions briefly with a smile, offer appropriate responses to keep the conversation flowing smoothly. Refrain from making derogatory remarks, as you wouldn't want others to question your words in your absence.

When it's your turn to bring up a topic, focus on something other than yourself and your interests. Try asking about what others are working on, thinking about, or if they have any new developments.

When you do speak, choose your words carefully. Share them sparingly and make sure they carry weight. Let your words flow naturally, without forcing them onto others.

#5 Practical Stoicism: Focus On the Essential

In your everyday life, as a citizen and individual, concentrate on the tasks at hand with grace and a genuine sense of care, freedom, and fairness. Set aside everything else. Find peace by approaching each aspect of your life as if it were your last, eliminating carelessness, objection to reason, hypocrisy, and self-esteem. Consider the insignificance of small things; by embracing them, you can lead a happy life, recalling the experiences of divine beings. The gods, after all, wouldn't bother with such trivial matters. (Marcus Aurelius)

Buddhists talk about the "monkey mind." It's that distracting voice in your head that becomes active when you're busy, prompting thoughts like, "I wonder if someone liked my Facebook post" or "I bet there's a new section in my newsfeed." Taming this inner voice is crucial. It constantly seeks distraction, jumping from one thing to another, always looking for something better. But if your mind is always in the future, you miss out on the present moment—the only moment that truly exists. Focus on each task as if it's important, and commit to completing it thoroughly. Live fully in the now, as that's where your existence truly resides.

Approach every chosen activity as if it holds significance. If you've decided to do something, work on it as if it could be your last opportunity on Earth. Treat each task with dedication, holding onto it until it's completed to your satisfaction. Immerse yourself in your work, experiencing it fully. Imagine death coming while you're doing the dishes—let it find you doing it perfectly. If it comes while you're driving, be firmly at the wheel. And if it finds you in bed, be content that you've made the most of your allotted time.

#6 Practical Stoicism: Get Up

If you struggle to get out of bed in the morning, remind yourself: "I need to go to work – as a human being. Why complain when I'm doing what I was born for – fulfilling my purpose? Was I made to stay snug under the covers and keep warm?"

So, were you born just to feel comfortable instead of actively doing and experiencing things? Have you not noticed the plants, birds, ants, spiders, and bees diligently carrying out their tasks and contributing to the order of the world? As a human, are you not ready to fulfill your role? Why not enthusiastically engage in what your nature calls for? - Marcus Aurelius

Similar to many aspects of life, excessive sleep can be harmful. Research indicates that sleeping more than 7 to 8 hours per day can lead to health issues like diabetes, obesity, headaches, back pain, and heart disease. Moreover, every extra hour of sleep beyond what your body needs for recovery is an hour lost forever.

That additional hour of sleep cannot be utilized for meditation, personal growth, or contributing to a better world. It won't challenge you or lead to significant accomplishments. You won't even remember what happened during that time. It becomes a precious moment lost in the sands of time, irreplaceable and gone for eternity.

It's more beneficial to reclaim that time and use it in accordance with your nature. You've rested enough; now is the time to take a deep breath and actively live your life.

#7 Practical Stoicism: Practicing Discomfort

Challenge yourself for a set number of days to accept the simplest and cheapest meals, wearing basic and rugged clothes, while asking yourself: "Is this the situation I feared?" - Seneca

In Stoic philosophy, building resilience is a key practice. The concept involves intentionally putting yourself in uncomfortable situations or enduring minor discomforts to better handle life's challenges with calmness. Stoics, along with other ancient Greek philosophers, were known to endure cold temperatures or wear uncomfortable attire as a way to toughen their minds. If you can train yourself to view small inconveniences as "indifferent," how much easier would it be to face larger challenges without fear?

Therefore, someone aspiring to be wise should regularly expose themselves to mild discomfort. Skip a day of indulging to test your willpower. Venture out on a chilly day with fewer layers to understand the weather. Leave the dinner table when there are still tempting dishes. Choose to park farther away and take a longer path inside. Turn off the hot water during a shower or switch off the air conditioner at home.

These small challenges act like exercises for your mental strength, hopefully leaving you more resilient when faced with significant tests in life.

#8 Practical Stoicism: Seek Your Consent

I often ponder how people prioritize seeking approval from others more than they value their own opinions. If you focus too much on looking good to please everyone, you'll likely compromise your approach to life. So, choose to be a philosopher, and if you wish to be seen in a certain light by someone, simply be yourself – that should be sufficient -
Epictetus

It's astonishing how many people willingly entrust their happiness, self-worth, and peace of mind to the opinions of others. Some believe they cannot be happy without someone's love or approval. They tirelessly seek validation from others, only to wonder why they are not receiving the satisfaction they crave.

You've taken a path that isn't leading you where you truly want to go. True happiness, a sense of fulfilment, and tranquillity cannot be handed to us by others. These feelings arise from our own actions and judgments. They are the rewards for living in accordance with our values, doing good deeds, and meeting our own standards. We have the power to achieve them by choosing to live wisely.

No one else can truly understand your journey and the efforts you've put in to reach where you are. It's impossible for them to know whether your achievements came from overcoming challenges or if they were handed to you easily. Did you resist temptation or give in? Did you stick to your values or follow what was popular? Did you face struggles to reach your goals, or did success come effortlessly? Did you achieve something meaningful through your strengths and weaknesses, or did you simply create an outwardly beautiful facade?

To find happiness, stop seeking pleasure in the opinions of others. Set your own standards of excellence and strive to meet them. No one in the world can help you achieve this – it's the only thing that truly matters.

#9 Practical Stoicism: Take a Sunrise

The Pythagoreans suggest observing the morning sky to reflect on celestial bodies that consistently follow their paths with purity and openness. Stars, unlike earthly objects, have no cover. (Marcus Aurelius)

Now and then, make the effort to rise before sunrise and position yourself where you can witness it. It won't take much time, and it's truly remarkable. Consider your position in the vast universe. Regardless of your past actions, each sunrise offers a fresh opportunity to make things right.

There's no guarantee that you'll witness another sunrise. Seize this chance wisely and make the most of it.

Stoic Principles

Stoic principles have become widely recognized as valuable goals, even making their way into the popular "Serenity Prayer" used in Twelve Step programs for overcoming addiction.

Here are eight fundamental ethical concepts embraced by Stoic philosophers:

Nature: Nature is rational.

Law of Reason: The universe follows the law of cause, and though humans can't escape its unstoppable force, they can consciously align with it in their unique way.

Virtue: Living in accordance with rational nature leads to a virtuous life.

Wisdom: Wisdom is the primary virtue, giving rise to essential qualities like intuition, courage, self-control, and justice.

Apathy: Since passion is irrational, life should be lived as a conscious struggle against intense emotions; they should be avoided.

Pleasure: Pleasure is neither inherently good nor bad. It is acceptable only if it doesn't interfere with the pursuit of virtue.

The Evil: Poverty, disease, and death are not inherently bad.

Duty: Virtue should not be pursued for the sake of pleasure but out of a sense of responsibility.

Modern Stoic philosopher Massimo Pigliucci describes Stoic philosophy as promoting a rigorous moral code. It encourages living in harmony with nature and under the guidance of virtue. Stoicism is seen as an ascetic system that advocates indifference to external factors (apathy) because, according to Stoics, nothing outside oneself can be inherently good or bad. Pain and pleasure, poverty and wealth, disease and health should be considered equally irrelevant in the pursuit of virtue.

11 Stoic Principles for a Happier and More Fulfilling Life

The quest for a joyful and meaningful life is central to our human experience. We all desire to lead a life that brings us a sense of satisfaction when we reflect upon it.

That's why I appreciate stoicism, an ancient philosophy well-known in Roman and Greek times, with notable thinkers like Marcus Aurelius and Seneca.

Stoicism has gained significant popularity recently, especially among entrepreneurs who value its practical principles.

> *Living a happy life requires very little; it's all about how you think and perceive things - Marcus Aurelius*

Stoicism primarily focuses on two key aspects: Happiness and Potential. These are the main things most of us are seeking. We aim to lead a content life while unlocking our full potential. Take a moment to ponder: if you achieve everything you've envisioned and can be happy, what more is there to pursue?

Here are eleven aloof rules that you can apply for an all the more satisfying life:

#1 Your Mind is Your Power

"You have control over your psyche, not outside events. Recognize this and find excellence." - Marcus Aurelius

One significant reason Stoicism has gained popularity is its connection to a mindset often born from thoughtful reflection.

This fundamental principle is closely tied to self-awareness. By managing your thoughts, you can lead a happier and more peaceful life. The key idea here is that your mind is the only thing you truly control. While you can try to influence external circumstances, this is often a challenging and inconsistent effort. If you focus on mastering your mind, you gain control over your life, tapping into a power greater than anything external to you.

#2 Time is Your Most Valuable Asset

"Don't live as if you have endless years ahead. Death casts a shadow over you. While you're alive and able, be rational."
- Marcus Aurelius

Although we logically grasp that our time is limited, our daily actions often go against this understanding. Many of us spend years in jobs we dislike, remain with people who don't bring us joy, and tolerate situations that leave us unsatisfied.

It's crucial to remind yourself regularly: time is your most precious resource. You only have a limited amount of it, and you must strive to live in a way that you won't regret.

#3 Live in the Present

"For me, the best proof of an organized mind is a person's ability to pause and spend some time in their own company." - Seneca

Being calm within yourself, staying present, and being aware of your surroundings indicate that you've put effort into cultivating a quality mind.

Interestingly, you can practice this without any special knowledge or training. Take a moment to be still with yourself. Notice the sensation of breath on your lips, the rise and fall of your chest, and the feelings in your body. Be aware of all the sensory experiences around you, like passing cars or bright lights.

Simply being in the present moment is a powerful experience with numerous benefits. Seize the opportunity.

#4 Appreciate What You Have

"Don't fantasize about having what you lack, but tally up the blessings you do have, and then, happily, reflect on how you'd yearn for them if they weren't yours." - Marcus Aurelius

Research now supports the benefits of gratitude, but Marcus Aurelius and other Stoics have long spoken about the power it holds.

Express gratitude for what you have. Not because it's everything or because you can't have more, but because cultivating gratitude transforms your mindset. Gratitude shifts your thinking from "I need," "I don't have enough," and "I wish I had" to "I'm so happy to have this," "I appreciate being," and "I'm content doing." The effort to make this change is minimal, but the positive impact on how you feel over time is tremendous.

#5 Remember the Purpose

Sustaining motivation involves having clear goals and reinforcing them daily. When pursuing a significant goal, understanding why you want it is crucial — knowing the purpose behind your efforts.

This isn't just about staying motivated when things are going well. It's about having a solid reason to keep going, especially when faced with challenges.

If getting out of bed is a struggle, remind yourself, "I need to go to work — as a person. Why complain when I'm doing what I was born for — fulfilling my purpose? Was I made for staying cozy under the covers?" – Marcus Aurelius.

Ask yourself: Were you born just to seek comfort instead of engaging in experiences and actions? Observe the plants, birds, ants, spiders, and bees diligently carrying out their tasks in the world. Are you not ready to fulfill your role as a human? Why not actively pursue what your nature requires?

The underlying message is that if you truly loved yourself, you would also love your nature and embrace what it demands from you.

#6 Seeking True Happiness Beyond Material Wealth

"Don't seek happiness in the material. Wealth does not consist in having large possessions, but in having few needs." - Epictetus

Excessive materialism is just another sign of what I call "emptiness" — the result of feeling like we lack something, something we often try to fill with material possessions.

The idea that material things bring us true fulfillment was created by advertisers aiming to sell more products. It's not grounded in scientific facts or research. While it may feel good temporarily when we acquire things we never had, this is a fleeting joy that can hardly be considered genuine happiness.

#7 Recognize the Source of Your Experiences

"See that everything we experience comes from within. Today I escaped fear. Or not, I rejected it because it was in me, in my perceptions - not outside." - Marcus Aurelius

It's easy to forget that everything we go through happens within the space between our ears—fear, anger, regret, joy, sadness, peace, thoughts, afterthoughts, stress, self-confidence, and everything else.

Our emotions shape our experiences, and based on these experiences, our brain decides how we respond emotionally.

When you understand that everything you experience originates from within, you'll realize you have more control than you think every day. Learning to manage your emotions gives you mastery over a great deal of happiness.

#8 Have a Role Model to Assess Your Character

Without a guide to compare yourself to, your path might not straighten out, much like a curve without a ruler. - Seneca

Pick someone whose way of life, words, and demeanor showcase a commendable personality. Consistently view this person as your guardian or a role model.

In my view, having someone as a benchmark is essential. It serves as a measuring stick against which your character can be evaluated.

Measuring your personal growth can be challenging without a way to gauge it. It's also not beneficial to compare yourself to Inividuals who aren't positive role models.

Identify someone who inspires you with their high character and embodies the qualities you admire. Once you've found such a person to strive towards, you'll have a meter to continually measure your progress.

#9 Shift Your Perspective on Mistakes

Ask yourself, does this situation prevent you from embodying virtues such as justice, generosity, self-control, reason, prudence, honesty, humility, and simplicity? – Marcus Aurelius

Instead of viewing mistakes negatively, consider them as opportunities for growth and self-improvement.

If traditional motivation and counselling methods fall short, focus on what you can control—your response and mindset. Marcus Aurelius encourages us to see challenges not as disgraceful events but as opportunities to demonstrate virtues. Embrace difficulties with the understanding that overcoming them is a stroke of luck.

It's natural to perceive bankruptcy or failure as unfavourable. However, instead of dwelling on the negative, see it as a step toward becoming the best version of yourself. Every setback is a chance for self-improvement, serving as a springboard for inevitable progress. In this light, view disappointments as extraordinary opportunities for personal growth and development.

#10 Employ What You've Penned Down

While books play a crucial role, it's a mistake to assume that you automatically embody the lessons. – Epictetus

Instead of just claiming to have read books, demonstrate that you've learned to think more effectively, become more discerning, and cultivate respect.

In our current era, acquiring knowledge and understanding various details is straightforward. However, the amount of information you possess doesn't necessarily translate to real-world action.

To put it simply, actively apply what you learn. You don't need to implement everything, but when you come across a valuable idea in a book or while writing, take thorough notes and devise a plan to integrate this new knowledge into your life.

#11 Consider How You Invest Your Time Wisely

It's better not to devote more time to trivial matters than they deserve. - Marcus Aurelius

An essential point to keep in mind: the significance of your attention depends on what you're focusing on.

Reflect on your daily activities. How much time do you allocate to what truly matters to you? Is it quality time with your family? Dedication to your profession? Taking care of your well-being?

Or do you find yourself spending hours on social media, gossip sites, or mindlessly scrolling through Reddit, only to realize that an entire hour has slipped away without any productive outcome?

Just like successful companies prioritize what matters most to them, ponder on how you utilize your time and make the necessary adjustments to turn your envisioned life into a reality.

The 10 Basic Principles and Beliefs

Stoicism guides you in maintaining a composed and resilient mindset, regardless of life's challenges. It empowers you to recognize and concentrate on things within your control, letting go of worries about things beyond your control.

However, this explanation only scratches the surface of Stoicism. In this initial section, my aim is to respond to your question, "What is it exactly?" I'll do so in a straightforward yet meaningful manner, emphasizing the fundamental principles that underlie Stoicism.

#1 Embracing the Stoic Way: Finding Fulfillment in Life

In the realm of ancient philosophy, there was a unanimous agreement among various schools that the ultimate purpose of life was termed as Eudaimonia. Now, defining Eudaimonia can be a bit tricky; think of it as the pinnacle of happiness and achievement—a life well-lived, full of vitality and regularity.

To break it down more simply, the equation of life's goal is essentially a good life multiplied by a wink. However, this may leave you wondering, "How does one actually go about living a good life?"

Enter Stoicism, with its core question: "How should we conduct our lives?" The Stoics, practical philosophers at heart, have developed numerous strategies for achieving a good life. We'll delve into these strategies in the upcoming principles, but first, let's understand how the Stoics succinctly expressed their life goal: "Live in harmony with nature."

This phrase, a concise maxim, serves as a daily reminder for Stoics. But what exactly does "living in harmony with nature" mean? That's the question we'll explore next.

Let's Hear Wisdom from Epictetus, a Key Stoic Guide:

"What is the purpose of a human being? A rational creature, susceptible to death." – Epictetus

Now, let's dig deeper and understand what distinguishes us from other creatures, like wild animals or sheep.

Epictetus warns against behaving like wild animals or sheep, as it jeopardizes our humanity. How do we mimic sheep-like behavior? It happens when we act impulsively, driven by our instincts or unruly emotions. Such actions, be they accidental, dirty, or ruthless, diminish our rationality—the very essence of what makes us human.

Being a human is more than just having unique physical characteristics. It's about possessing social and mental strengths, particularly the ability to reason and create interesting things. Our distinctiveness lies in our rationality.

So, what does "living in harmony with nature" mean in practical terms? It means acting rationally, not impulsively or instinctively, as animals do. We should always engage our natural ability to reason in all our actions. When we act with reason, we align ourselves with nature and fulfill our human potential.

In essence, we must avoid behaving like animals, tapping into our unique gift of reason. This aligns with the Stoic idea of "living by virtue," which encapsulates their vision for a meaningful life. Now, let's explore this Stoic principle further to gain a clearer understanding of how it manifests in our everyday lives.

#2 Beyond Power: Flourishing through Virtue

In the Stoic perspective, life's ultimate achievement is not about wielding power but embodying the highest good through right conduct – leading a life marked by success. Let's break down this concept.

For Stoics, "virtue" signifies exceptional behavior aligned with our rational human nature, essentially living the good life. Expressing the best of ourselves involves embodying virtues in various ways. Stoics identified **four cardinal virtues**:

Wisdom or Prudence: This encompasses excellent reasoning, common sense, perspective, and practical wisdom.

Justice or Equity: Involves kindness, benevolence, public service, and fair relations.

Courage or Firmness: Encompasses bravery, perseverance, authenticity (honesty), and trust.

Self-discipline or Temperance: Involves order, self-control, forgiveness, and humility.

By consistently practicing these virtues, one can attain a good life or Eudaimonia – the highest life goal for Stoics. The key to a virtuous life lies in perfecting these qualities and living in accordance with them.

Being virtuous, in the Stoic sense, requires practicing all virtues simultaneously. Acting courageously all day but succumbing to excesses at night, for example, would not be true virtue, as it violates the virtue of self-discipline. Virtue, for Stoics, is an all-or-nothing package.

Stoics understood that virtue should be its own reward. Doing the right thing becomes valuable in itself, aligning with nature, reason, and the cardinal virtues. The nature of your actions matters less than the fact that they align with virtue on your journey to a good life.

The Stoic emphasis on doing the right thing stems from the character and the use of reason in a beneficial and commendable manner. It revolves around who you are and the actions you take.

While acting virtuously may bring additional benefits, such as feeling happy for acting justly, these outcomes are viewed as "extra bonuses." They shouldn't be the primary motivation for virtuous actions, as they are not entirely within our control.

So, the Stoic advice is clear: always use reason and strive to do the right thing. Act in accordance with the virtues of practical wisdom, justice, courage, and self-discipline. The outcomes of your virtuous actions may not be fully under your control, and therefore, should not be the sole reason for your actions. This principle sets the stage for the next Stoic theory.

#3 Direct Your Focus: Mastering What's in Your Power

"Use what's in your power and take the rest when it happens. Some things are with us, and others are not with us." - Epictetus.

This statement by Epictetus, found at the beginning of the Enchiridion of Epictetus, is crucial for understanding Stoic philosophy. It introduces the fundamental principle of Stoicism known as the "stoic division of control."

The core idea is to discern what "depends on us" or is within our power and what is beyond our control. We have the ability to make voluntary decisions, take actions, and pass judgments, but many other aspects lie outside our control.

Consider your body as an example. While you can adopt healthy habits like following a nutritious diet and exercising regularly, factors such as genetics, early exposure, experiences, diseases, and injuries are beyond your control.

Stoicism encourages us to focus on what we can control and acknowledge the limitations of what we cannot. You can have a general overview of what lies within your influence and what doesn't.

For instance, while you may aspire to achieve a healthy and attractive body, recognize that there are limits to this control. You can manage your actions, but factors like genes and external circumstances are not entirely under your command.

The key to finding contentment lies in accepting the outcomes with equanimity. Satisfaction and trust come from knowing you've done your best within your capabilities. Whether the results meet your expectations or not, the focus is on the effort you put in.

This approach boosts confidence. By giving your all to what you can control, you enter challenging moments with assurance, having done your utmost. If the outcome falls short, you can gracefully accept it, saying, "Well, I did my best."

This philosophy has proven effective for many. The success lies in concentrating on what you can control and embracing what you cannot. It's about expressing yourself honestly, knowing you've either excelled in your efforts or recognized areas where improvement is needed.

The things you let go of, like your thoughts and actions, hold the utmost importance in life. Donald Robertson eloquently expresses this idea in his book "Stoicism and the Image of Happiness":

"The key insight of this philosophy is that the primary good, the most important thing in life, must be 'based on us,' and it's also the most challenging and noble aspect of integrity. It makes us wholly responsible for the most significant aspect of life, removing any excuse for not thriving and obtaining the best life possible, as this is always within our reach."

In essence, the most appealing aspect of Stoicism lies in the recognition that our prosperity is our responsibility because everything crucial in life depends on us.

The main takeaway is to focus your attention and efforts on what you have control over, and then allow the universe to handle the rest. The Stoics used the analogy of archery to illustrate this point:

Imagine archers aiming for a target. Many factors are within their control, such as training, selecting the arrow, aiming, and deciding when to release it. They can give their best effort until the arrow leaves their bow.

Now, will it hit the target? External factors like the wind, sudden target movements, or obstacles between the arrow and the target can come into play. The Stoic practitioner is prepared to accept any outcome with ease because they have done their best and left the uncontrollable aspects to nature.

This concept resonates with modern soccer. How often do players miss a free-kick and then express frustration at the unfavorable outcome? Not too often.

"The power of Stoicism lies in internalizing the fundamental truth that we can control our behavior, but not its results – let alone the results of other people's behaviors. This realization leads to a peaceful acceptance of whatever happens, knowing that we've done our best in the given circumstances."

It's impressive, isn't it? And what can we always strive for? Living in harmony with virtue. We can always aim to use reason, act boldly, treat others fairly, and exercise moderation.

"Practice immediately saying to every strong impression: 'An impression is all you are, not the source of the impression.' Test and evaluate it based on your criteria, but

first ask: 'Is it something that is or is not under my control?'
- Epictetus

Examine your impressions and determine if you have a choice. If it's within your control, take action. If not, accept it as it is. This concept leads us directly to the next significant Stoic idea."

#4 Understanding the Value of Things in Stoic Philosophy

Stoic philosophy introduces a clear distinction among things — labeling them as "good," "bad," or "indifferent."

Good things: These are the fundamental virtues — wisdom, righteousness, courage, and self-discipline. Conversely, bad things encompass the contradictions of these virtues, namely the four vices of madness, injustice, cowardice, and tolerance.

Indifferent things: This category includes everything else, such as life and death, fame and bad reputation, pleasure and pain, wealth and poverty, health and disease. Notably, indifferent things can be summarized as health, prosperity, and reputation.

What stands out is that Stoic philosophy considers indifferent things, often judged as good or bad by ordinary people, as not significantly contributing to or hindering our development as rational beings. In Stoicism, these indifferent things do not play a crucial role in leading a good life.

In essence, indifferent things like health, prosperity, and reputation are entirely neutral to the concept of a good life. They aren't inherently good or bad; they are simply neutral. Whether one is rich or poor, healthy or sick, these factors are not essential for perfect happiness. The lesson here is to learn to be "indifferent to indifferent things" and find contentment with what nature presents to us.

It's important to clarify that indifference, in this context, doesn't imply a lack of emotion. In fact, Stoics argue that since indifferent things don't depend on us, they are pursued by something greater than us, and we can love them in the same way. Being indifferent to indifferent things means accepting them as they are and embracing them with love.

But what if our health is better than illness? Yes, while indifferent things cannot be inherently "good," some are considered more valuable and preferable. The Stoics introduced the concepts of indifferent "preferred" and "dispreferred" things.

The logic behind this is straightforward. Positively indifferent things like good health, friendship, prosperity, and good looks are categorized as favorite indifferent things, while their opposites are considered indifferent.

Does this distinction make sense? Absolutely. The Stoics aimed to make a harmonious and Eudaimonian life achievable for everyone, regardless of social status, health, wealth, or appearance. Although these qualities are preferred, the Stoics emphasize that they are still indifferent and unnecessary for leading a virtuous life. The ultimate goal is not the pursuit of these preferred things but the cultivation of virtue and the achievement of a flourishing life.

People naturally seek joy over pain, prosperity over poverty, and health over disease. However, the Stoics advise pursuing these things with integrity and virtue. In other words, it's better to endure pain, poverty, or disease honorably than to seek joy, prosperity, or health in a way that compromises your principles.

Consider some examples: Friendship, according to Stoicism, is indifferent; it's better to have friends, but when faced with decisions involving a friend or upholding good character, the Stoics prioritize the right attitude. For them, justice holds more weight than friendship.

Always keep in mind that while some things may be preferred, they are ultimately indifferent to achieving a good life. The only unequivocally positive thing, according to Stoicism, is virtue—comprising wisdom, courage, justice, and self-discipline—which is entirely within our control. On the flip side, the only unequivocally negative thing is vice—madness, cowardice, injustice, and tolerance—which also depends entirely on us.

Everything else falls into the category of indifferent. In the grand scheme of a good life, these indifferent factors don't matter because they don't depend on us. So, what you have or don't have isn't crucial; what truly matters is what you do with it. Your actions are the sole aspect under your control.

While it's preferable to be rich and healthy, what's important to the Stoics is how you behave in any given situation. Your behavior, guided by virtue, is the crux of Stoic philosophy and leads us to the next key Stoic principle.

#5 Take Action - Embracing Stoic Philosophy as a Warrior of the Mind

Can I really make a difference in my life? This question is crucial for Stoics because they recognize that most things are beyond their control, and they aim to approach them with indifference. But does this mean sitting idly, doing nothing, and caring about nothing?

The Stoics dismiss such a notion, referring to it as the "lazy argument." In the words of Donald Robertson, "Events aren't predestined to unfold a certain way regardless of your actions; they unfold in conjunction with what you do."

Your actions are within your control. Doing nothing won't lead to a good life or make you a better person, according to Stoic philosophy. While external events are viewed as indifferent, the Stoics are far from indifferent about their own actions.

Living in accordance with virtue to attain a flourishing life requires the Stoics to consistently strive to "do the right thing." It's not merely about contemplating how to live but actively implementing these ideas in the world. For Stoic students, it's not enough to theorize about making a living; they must venture into the world and put their ideas into practice. A good life is earned by taking the right actions.

The Stoics emphasize that it's not sufficient to grasp abstract ideas about how to live; one must vigorously apply these concepts. Mere knowledge and talk are ineffective without practical application. Neglecting to apply what is learned can lead to contradictory actions.

Donald Robertson aptly compares the true philosopher to a "warrior of the spirit" in his book on Cognitive Behavioral Therapy. In ancient times, a philosopher, literally a "lover of wisdom," was seen as a warrior of the spirit. Such an individual engaged in battles within their own mind, striving for self-control and dedicating themselves to intellectual exercises.

Contrastingly, in contemporary times, the philosopher has transformed into a more reserved figure—a custodian of knowledge. Instead of fighting battles, the modern philosopher collects ideas as theoretical knowledge, storing them in the mind. However, this approach often neglects the essential aspect of living out these ideas.

"Even if we speak fluently in class, we retire to practice and are miserably devastated." - Epictetus

The Stoic philosophy encourages individuals not to remain passive but to decide to be a warrior and put Stoic principles into practice.

An accessible way to start this practice is by embracing the concept of practicing misfortune.

#6 Embracing Challenges - Anticipate, "What Could Possibly Go Wrong?"

Let's think about vaccines. What's their purpose? It's simple: vaccines prepare your body to fight diseases before they actually attack.

In a similar fashion, the Stoics developed a mental tool, a kind of vaccination against misfortune. They mentally prepared themselves for the possibility of something bad happening. This preparation was a key aspect of studying Stoic philosophy—getting ready for future events to maintain calmness in the face of adversity.

"The Stoics trained to maintain equanimity and freedom from emotional suffering by presenting themselves regularly and preparing to face them well in advance," - Donald Robertson.

Now, let's explore one of the most valuable tools in the Stoic arsenal: the practice of adversity. William Irvine, author of "A Guide to the Good Life," describes it as "the most valuable technique in the Stoics Toolkit" and labels it as "negative visualization." Here, "bad luck" isn't inherently bad; it's considered completely indifferent.

The Stoics aim to strengthen this indifference toward feared outcomes. This way, they can confront challenges calmly, rationally, and patiently when they eventually arise. The practice involves asking, "What could possibly go wrong?" and mentally preparing oneself for potential adversity.

Consider this scenario: You're gearing up for a weekend getaway. The night before, you've booked your seat, packed your bags, and prepped the car. You have a plan, and you're all set. Now, throw a curveball at yourself – ask, "What could go wrong?"

Anticipate things not going exactly as planned. Have a backup strategy. What if something unexpected occurs? So, if this and that happen... What if... Then I... What if... Then I...

"Nothing happens to the sage against his expectations." - Seneca

This mindset prepares you mentally for any situation. It doesn't mean you'll magically find bad things bearable, but it helps you keep your composure when challenges arise. You can face adversities with a calmer demeanor, analyze them rationally, and take intelligent actions.

> *"I might wish to be free from torture, but when the time comes, I will bear it with courage and honor. Wouldn't I rather not go to war? But if war should happen to me, I want injuries, hunger, and others. Honor the needs of war. I'm not even so mad about the disease, but when I get sick, I don't want to do anything reckless or dishonest. It's not about wanting these adversities, but about virtue, bearable adversities." - Seneca*

Seneca emphasizes that desiring life's difficulties would be absurd. However, it's equally foolish to believe they won't happen. Prepare for difficulties to be ready to face them instead of being caught off guard.

Stoic Premeditation involves imagining potential challenging scenarios in advance, so you're not taken by surprise and can respond with composure and virtuous action.

"No desolation - the feeling that we are totally depressed and shocked by an event - is a factor in that it is unlikely that we have even considered that event." - Ryan Holiday

Consider the brilliance of this. Reflecting on my first breakup, if I had thought about it happening (which was very likely), it would still have been tough, but I would have been more prepared to cope with it.

In essence, deliberately contemplating adversity helps you face real challenges with greater strength and resilience. As Donald

Robertson notes, "Psychological resilience tends to generalize in such a way that even situations that are neither anticipated nor studied directly can be perceived as less overwhelming as long as a host of other adversities are resiliently anticipated and overcome."

So, what could possibly go wrong in the next few days?

 # 7 Include a Contingency in Your Planned Promotions

Recall that virtue is considered the highest good and that our control extends solely to our actions. These principles are pivotal to what Stoics refer to as the "reserve clause."

As students of Stoicism, we strive to act virtuously and give our best effort, all the while acknowledging that the outcome is not entirely within our direct influence.

Seneca articulates the reserve clause with the expression:

"I intend to do it, as long as nothing arises to hinder my decision." **To illustrate, he offers an example:** *"I will board the ship if no unforeseen obstacles arise."*

Fortunately, Seneca was remarkably resilient.

Here's the key to bolstering your self-confidence: (1) strive to excel, (2) recognize that results are beyond your absolute control, (3) embrace whatever outcome unfolds, and finally, (4) persist in acting virtuously.

In essence, we formulate a plan and exert our utmost effort to achieve our objectives. Simultaneously, we acknowledge that unforeseen circumstances may intervene, preventing us from reaching our goals. We accept these realities, adapt our plans accordingly, and persist in striving for our best despite challenges.

This approach is often referred to as a process. In sports, for instance, the focus is on the process—your efforts, struggles, training, readiness, and all the elements you can control, with results being a byproduct. The ultimate aim is not merely winning but becoming the best version of yourself.

It's crucial to understand that not controlling the outcome doesn't imply detachment; rather, it emphasizes concentrating on actions that can positively influence the result.

There are times when things may not go as planned, even when we invest our best efforts and truly deserve success. Regardless of the outcome, we can always take pride in giving our best.

Massimo Pigliucci eloquently states in his book, "How to Be a Stoic": "The distinguishing features of a wise person lie in their efforts, which, although well-founded, are not confused with the workings of the universe."

This Stoic concept is truly profound—act with a reserve clause, introduce a constraint, and then embrace (or even love) whatever unfolds.

Recall the Stoic archers? They shoot at the target, giving their best, and then accept the outcome with equanimity. This acceptance of reality leads us to the next Stoic principle.

8 Cupid Fati - Loves Everything That Happens

"Don't insist that things unfold according to your desires. Instead, embrace events as they unfold naturally, and your life will take a positive turn." - Epictetus

This quote is a personal favorite of mine, serving as a guide to a content and happy life. Imagine something unexpected occurs – what's easier to change, the event itself or our perspective on it? The answer is clear. Events are in the past, unchangeable. However, our mindset is flexible. This is what sports enthusiasts might call the "art of understanding," and Stoicism terms it accepting everything without resistance.

Ryan Holiday added in The Daily Stoic:

"And the expert stoics go further. Instead of simply accepting what is happening, they ask us to really enjoy what happened, whatever it is. Many centuries later, Nietzsche coined the perfect expression to capture this idea: Amor fati (a love of destiny). Not only do you understand it, but you also love everything that happens. "

Breaking it down, we can see it in two stages:

Acknowledgment: Recognizing that we can't control every happening and that it's okay. Another force shaped the moment, and we just need to grasp that fact.

Embracing: Moving beyond acceptance to actually loving everything that unfolds. Someone else crafted the moment; our role is to enjoy it.

It's quite normal to feel hesitant about expressing gratitude for something we dislike. Here's a helpful perspective: consider the powerful force that shapes the world and influences every event. All occurrences, whether wanted or unexpected, are specifically meant for you. In the moment, things might seem unfavorable, but there's a larger purpose that you may not grasp yet, and it will ultimately work in your favor.

Expressing gratitude for something undesired may seem awkward, but try to think of the influential force that guides the world's happenings. All events, whether you prefer them or not, unfold with your benefit in mind. While an occurrence may initially seem unfavorable, there's a greater purpose that you might not comprehend immediately, leading to long-term advantages.

Instead of resisting what has happened, acknowledge that it has occurred and happened for a reason.

Think of it like a dog on a leash attached to a moving cart. The leash allows the dog to choose between two options: (1) go with the flow, enjoying the ride and exploring the surroundings despite the lack of control over the direction of the cart, or (2) stubbornly resist, yet still be dragged along for the journey.

We are like this dog; we can either make the most of the journey or resist every decision made by the cart. One path is easy and joyful, while the other is tiring and miserable. The choice is yours—the metaphor of the dog and the cart.

The cart keeps moving; change is inevitable. To quote Ryan Holiday: "Being angry about things is wrong to assume they will last" Accepting the direction and speed of the cart doesn't mean giving up. As Ryan Holiday puts it, "It has nothing to do with action - this is for things that are immune to action. It is much easier to talk about how things should be. It takes tenacity, humility, and will. Accept them for what they really are."

Be a resilient individual, taking things as they come and making the best of them. Be like a wise dog enjoying the trip, even if the cart takes a challenging route.

9 Turn Obstacles into Opportunities: Perception is Key what is Perception?

Understanding perception is crucial in navigating life's challenges. Perception is how we interpret and make decisions about the events around us. Picture it as either a burdensome lead ball, dragging us down, or a potent potion, strengthening us.

In Stoic philosophy, events are not labeled as inherently good or bad; they are considered indifferent. What truly matters is our judgment of these events.

> *"If something external causes you pain, it's not the thing itself but your judgment of it that hurts. And you have the power to change that judgment right now." - Marcus Aurelius*

This principle puts you in control of your life. You may not dictate external events, but you can shape how you perceive and respond to them. Ultimately, everything starts to make sense.

Our emotional state is not dictated by events; it's driven by our judgments of those events. Consider a rainy day – an external occurrence. Luke may see it as an obstacle to his beach plans, Farmer Ben might rejoice, anticipating a good harvest, and Aunt Charlize could be upset about her laundry in the rain. The rain itself isn't the cause of joy or suffering; it's the individual judgments that vary.

Stoics aimed to avoid being swayed by initial impressions of external events, acknowledging their lack of control over such occurrences. Instead, they strived to (1) objectively assess events and (2) respond in the best way possible.

When something happens, our initial impression is automatic and often beyond our control. However, we have a choice in whether to accept or challenge that initial impression. Stoicism encourages us to scrutinize our impressions by asking, "What exactly happened?" and then objectively observing the event, perhaps imagining how it might appear to someone else.

For example, if a friend accidentally breaks a glass during dinner, we may dismiss it as inconsequential. Yet, if we break the same glass, our judgment becomes harsher – labeling it as bad, embarrassing, or negligent.

So, the Stoic approach involves objectively assessing events: It's raining, the glass is broken – and then consciously choosing our best response.

"Keep in mind that setbacks may affect your body or possessions, but your mind remains within your control, ready to transform adversity into happiness through virtuous responses." - Epictetus

You always have the power to react positively. Every situation can be viewed as a chance to respond with a constructive mindset. For instance, I recall a time when my younger brother consistently annoyed me. Instead of letting it bother me, viewing him as a perpetual annoyance, I could have seen him as a valuable training partner, helping me cultivate patience, integrity, and kindness. Unfortunately, I allowed myself to get angry, spreading negativity.

Consider your recent plans. How have they been disrupted? How can you turn these challenges into an opportunity to practice virtue or another form of excellence?

"The obstacle to action advances action. What is in the middle becomes the way." - Marcus Aurelius

The Stoics advocated for turning obstacles into opportunities. Stoics saw challenges as chances to thrive despite unfavorable circumstances.

Perception is crucial in recognizing these opportunities. How you see things matters more than the things themselves. Stoicism encourages us to view everything as a chance for personal growth. This mindset allows us to transform both obstacles and blessings into opportunities for progress.

Certainly, life can be tough at times. It's not about wearing rose-colored glasses and pretending everything is fine when faced with profound loss, such as the death of a loved one. Challenges happen, and we must acknowledge them. However, we have a choice – we can bury our heads in the sand or actively seek opportunities within adversity, using them to the best of our abilities.

Yet, there's a hurdle. Before we can question our initial reactions and find opportunities, we must be aware of our impressions as they happen. We need to be vigilant first.

10 Be Mindful - Stoic Awareness is Where It All Starts

If you aspire to live by Stoic philosophy, being mindful is where it all begins. To live a life of strength and reason, incorporating wisdom, courage, honesty, and moderation, paying close attention to your actions is crucial. Without this awareness, how can you consistently choose the rational practices needed for such a life?

In essence, Stoic principles emphasize a profound understanding akin to great science. What does it entail? Essentially, it involves monitoring your thoughts and actions, being fully present in the here and now. It means knowing and understanding your actions at all times. Whether you're focusing on what you can control, crafting the right response, or managing your impressions, constant mindfulness is essential.

Stoic awareness is a fundamental aspect of practicing Stoicism, and it's a skill that develops through regular practice. It goes both ways – being aware helps you step back from your thoughts, enabling you to consciously choose the best course of action instead of merely reacting on autopilot.

When you experience an emotion, it's crucial to recognize that emotion at that very moment. Only then can you decide if the emotion serves a purpose or if there's a better way to respond. If you're not aware that you're acting based on emotions, it becomes extremely challenging to make conscious choices and alter your behavior.

Stoicism requires a certain level of awareness. Donald Robertson emphasizes the importance of Stoics paying attention to their will, as voluntary thoughts and actions are the only things entirely under one's control.

In practical terms, we jeopardize our philosophy and Stoic principles when we react without being mindful, engaging in actions without realizing what we're doing. For instance, getting frustrated with a driver during the daily commute, being consumed by thoughts of an annoying client during lunch, or losing composure while watching a football game with friends.

During such moments, we lose our detachment, and regaining awareness can take time, with the risk of not even realizing our irrational behavior.

This is why the Stoics advocate for daily reflection practices, such as the evening retrospective. Seneca, for example, reflected on his day before bedtime, acknowledging his actions, assessing what went well, and contemplating improvements.

Before going to bed, take a few minutes to think about your day. Consider what you did well and what needs improvement. Reflect on your actions, asking questions like: What can I do better? How can I be the best version of myself? What changes would I like to make? By doing this consistently, you not only enhance your self-awareness but also train your mind to be more conscious throughout the day.

Marcus Aurelius, the Roman Emperor, wrote his thoughts in a similar manner, reflecting privately on his day. So, by jotting down your reflections, who knows, maybe people will be reading them in two thousand years.

Stoic Love for Humanity

Stoic philosophy acknowledges our social nature, emphasizing a genuine warmth and inclination toward others. This forms the basis of stoic philanthropy, which is a rational love for our fellow beings in the universe. Essentially, humans are both rational and social beings.

While Stoics understand that friendships and relationships are ultimately indifferent, they highly value them. Stoics prefer to live with friends, neighbors, and roommates, but they don't consider these relationships as necessary for a good life. They can lead a fulfilled life without close connections, but they choose not to because of their natural affection for humanity and the belief that virtues like justice and courage are better exercised in interactions with others.

In the words of Marcus Aurelius,

"We should do good to others as effortlessly as a horse runs or a vine produces grapes without dwelling on the fruit it bears."

It's our human instinct to do good, and Marcus suggests that all our actions should be for the benefit of everyone, without worrying about others' reactions. This concept aligns with the idea that even emperors should prioritize the common good over personal interests.

However, there is a limit – the primary reason for promoting the common good is the virtue of justice. Living in harmony with virtue benefits both ourselves and others. As Rudolf Steiner noted, "If the rose enhances itself, it enhances the garden."

Marcus Aurelius emphasizes the idea that humans are born to perform acts of kindness and serve the common good. Doing benevolent acts is fulfilling our purpose, and the intrinsic reward is in the virtuous action itself. In summary, the Stoic principle is to do good without expecting anything in return, understanding that virtue is its own reward.

What if others engage in wrongful actions?

The Stoics held the belief that no one intentionally commits wrongdoing; rather, people act based on their own understanding. According to Massimo Pigliucci, the wrongdoer often lacks knowledge of what is truly beneficial, a concept known as amathia. The Stoics argue that what is good for an individual is the same for everyone, providing sufficient reason to enhance social well-being.

When someone commits an act for their own benefit, the Stoic perspective advises against blaming them. Instead, they suggest feeling compassion towards them. Epictetus emphasizes this sentiment by likening it to pitying the blind or the lame, extending the compassion to those impaired in their moral judgment. Those who hold onto this understanding, as Epictetus points out, won't harbor anger, resentment, accusations, hatred, or offenses towards others.

Avoid harboring hatred towards wrongdoers, for they may not possess a better understanding. It becomes your responsibility as you perceive yourself as a role model to act in the right way, not only for others but primarily for your own well-being. Your actions matter significantly, as they define your character. Therefore, focus on doing what is right, and in doing so, you contribute to the betterment of both yourself and those around you.

Advantages of a Stoic Practice

Stoicism, with a history dating back over thirty-two centuries, offers valuable insights to help individuals break free from unnecessary worries about things beyond their control and cultivate a positive life outlook. While the external aspects of contemporary life differ significantly from a hundred or even two thousand years ago, our internal struggles have remained remarkably similar. In the present era, marked by social media, advanced technology, and conveniences unimaginable to past emperors, people still grapple with impatience, concerns about others' opinions, and difficulties in coping with change.

In the face of rapid technological advancements and increasing uncertainties in various aspects of life, from employment to environmental challenges, it becomes evident that individuals of all backgrounds can derive substantial benefits from embracing Stoic principles. By learning to think more clearly, reducing anxiety, and optimizing resource utilization in the coming year, anyone can enhance their well-being in today's fast-paced world.

With that understanding, here are seven advantages of incorporating Stoic practices into your life.

#1 You Won't Worry About What Others Think

"Get rid of your concern for public opinion—it's always uncertain and divided." - Seneca

One of the most challenging things a person can do is not be swayed by the opinions of others. It's tough because it involves disregarding the viewpoints of those you care about and who care about you. It also means living life on your own terms, based on what you believe is right. Choosing to live according to your principles requires taking responsibility for your actions and not postponing essential tasks to your future self. It might seem easier to just do what others suggest, as it allows you to shift blame to those you've listened to if things go wrong.

"Being everywhere means being nowhere." – Seneca.

Avoiding responsibility for decisions often leaves us dissatisfied with ourselves. When we fail to think for ourselves and act based on what is good and true, mistakes made by following the world's advice can lead to bitterness and anger. However, making mistakes based on our own judgments provides an opportunity to learn and grow. Recognize that people, especially those close to you, will always have opinions about your appearance or choices. While some may think it's helpful, trying to follow all these conflicting opinions can lead your mind in a thousand different directions.

Instead, we must make a conscious effort to seek the truth and align our lives with it. We should also trust our judgment so that when we consider the opinions of others, we ensure they align with our values rather than just satisfying our ears. This way, we can not only regain our self-esteem but also better serve our fellow human beings.

#2 You Will Use Your Time Wisely

"We should conduct ourselves as if we are at the end of our lives. Let nothing be left unsettled. Strive to maintain a balance in the ledger of life every day... Always time enough." - Seneca

In the last hundred years, death has become less pervasive. However, in the past, people were surrounded by mortality, witnessing the deaths of parents, friends, and siblings due to wars and plagues. In 1900, the infant mortality rate exceeded 150 per 1,000 children. This constant exposure to death served as a stark reminder of the fleeting nature of life.

While this reality may evoke sadness for some, Stoics see it as an opportunity to make each day count. By approaching life as if it were finite, they find contentment in knowing they are making the most of their time. Acknowledging that every action might be the last has the effect of making life feel more vivid and significant. Imagine knowing that tomorrow might be the last time you see your spouse, father, or best friend alive—how would you spend that time? The Stoics suggest focusing on meaningful connections, avoiding trivial concerns, and ensuring you savor each moment.

Stoics recognize that we don't have to wait until the end of our lives to fully enjoy life.

"Consider yourself dead. You have lived your life. Now take what is left and steer it in the right direction." – Marcus Aurelius

This approach isn't about inducing sadness or advocating reckless behavior. Instead, it serves as a reminder to live a fulfilling life, minimizing time spent on trivial matters and being fully present in the here and now.

#3 You Will Focus on What You Can Control

"The main task in life is simply to identify and separate things so that we can clearly say which external factors are not under my control and which have to do with the decisions I control. So, where do I look for good and bad? Not to the uncontrollable appearances, but in myself to the decisions that are mine." - Epictetus

We all carry hopes, dreams, fears, and frustrations. We hope to land our dream jobs, and we fear that it might not happen. The influences of our education, current values, and the people around us can often cloud our judgment. Life can be challenging, and if you look around, it's easy to find evidence that supports these challenges. However, just because we find things that confirm our frustrations doesn't make those frustrations automatically valid.

The core practice of Stoicism is to remember what is within our control and what is not. This means that the things causing frustration are not inherently frustrating; they are just things, and it is we who feel the frustration. The Stoics understood that relinquishing control over things beyond their reach would disturb their peace of mind. By giving up their power over what truly mattered— their own reactions—they surrendered their tranquillity.

Recognizing that dwelling on things beyond our control hinders us from directing our energy towards what we can control is crucial. Instead of battling frustration over not being as humorous as desired, following Marcus Aurelius' advice, you should focus on "...those traits that are entirely in your power: sincerity, gravity, persistence in work, aversion to pleasure, contentment with your part, and a simple life..." Concentrating on what you can control while letting go of what you cannot will lead to a happier, more robust, and more effective life.

#4 You Will Reduce Distractions

"If a person does not find deep meaning, he likes to get distracted." - Viktor E. Frankl

Avoiding distractions has become more challenging than ever. Numerous tempting options are available, often beyond the reach of most people. It seems that everyone worldwide is vying for our attention. Individuals want us to listen to their podcasts, companies want us to view their ads to promote their products, and networks want us to watch their TV shows. Everyone is competing for a slice of our time, and the list is endless. The more connected we become, the more we crave constant engagement. It's a perpetual cycle, all aimed at preventing us from being alone with our thoughts and avoiding boredom.

The issue is that the same things keeping us from getting bored also hinder our personal growth. While playing a game on your phone might initially seem like a way to stave off boredom, in the long run, it distracts you from your emotions. By avoiding experiencing your feelings, you miss out on valuable learning opportunities. For instance, if something upsets you, and your immediate reaction is to reach for your phone and scroll through Instagram, you are preventing yourself from learning from that moment of frustration.

#5 You Will Overcome Your Fears

"He suffers more than necessary who suffers before it is necessary." - Seneca

Fear is more prevalent today than ever. We often feel uneasy about not doing what we should, leading to constant worry about the past, neglecting the present, and fearing the future. Dealing with fear is undoubtedly challenging, but it becomes even more difficult when we haven't learned to overcome it. Epictetus offers a straightforward solution: identify what you can control, take action, and let go of the rest. While easier said than done, consider how unproductive it is to fear the future when there's much you can do in the present. The future is uncertain, and the only place where we can make a difference is now.

"True happiness is enjoying the present without anxious dependence on the future, not getting carried away by hopes or fears, but resting contentedly because those who desire nothing are fortunate. The greatest blessing for humanity lies within us and is within our reach. A wise person is content with their destiny, whatever it may be, without longing for what they lack." - Seneca

The challenge lies in not taking the time to differentiate between things we control and those we don't. This often leads us to act blindly and unintentionally, worrying about things that don't warrant concern. By understanding what is beyond our control, we can find ways to cultivate peace and tranquility.

#6 You Will Appreciate More

"All you need is this: the certainty of judgment in the present moment, action for the common good at the present moment, and an attitude of gratitude in the present moment for all that hinders you." - Marcus Aurelius

As the emperor of the Roman Empire, Marcus Aurelius faced constant challenges that most of us can't relate to, both professionally and personally. The weight of an empire at war rested on his shoulders, and his son was a disappointment. Despite these difficulties, Marcus remained grateful for every circumstance he encountered, whether good or bad. This mindset empowered him to act virtuously even when others might crumble under the emperor's pressure.

Marcus viewed every challenge and setback as an opportunity for personal growth. He believed that these challenges prepared him for life's ultimate test – death. This sentiment is evident in his meditations: "Walk in harmony with nature throughout this short period, gracefully reaching your final resting place, like a ripe olive falling and praising the earth that nourished it. Give thanks to the tree from which it grew." Marcus understood that by choosing gratitude over anger, one can experience greater peace and satisfaction, even in the face of challenges.

#7 I Prefer Having Less

"A man is not rich because he has more money, but because he needs less; he who is content is truly wealthy." - Seneca

Often, we compare ourselves to others, thinking that they are happier or have more than we do. However, in this comparison, we tend to forget that we already possess everything necessary for a healthy, happy, and strong life. Seneca, in one of his famous letters, advised his friend Lucius to occasionally live in a simpler way — eating basic foods and wearing rough clothes. The purpose was to show that living with less is not something to fear. Seneca suggests that practicing simplicity allows us to recognize that we can be content without constantly desiring more. The feeling of "lack" is often just a perception, and it fades away when you realize that you can lead a happy life without certain things. To truly be rich, you don't need to fear losing possessions because you already have all you need.

It's time to strengthen your inner resilience

"The universe is in flux, and life is a matter of perspective." -
Marcus Aurelius

While we may not know what the future holds, we can equip ourselves to face uncertainty with strength and triumph. Stoic philosophy doesn't promise constant happiness, but it teaches us to do what is right. By choosing the right actions, we can withstand the inevitable changes and challenges life throws our way. Change is the only certainty in life, and practicing stoicism, with objective judgment, gratitude, and resilience, prepares us to navigate through it successfully.

CHAPTER 5: HOW TO BECOME A MODERN STOIC?

Stoicism has been around for a long time and has been a part of Western thought for quite a while. However, it has gained renewed interest for various reasons:

Information Overflow: We now generate more information in a week than in the first thousands of years of human existence. Ideas spread quickly and easily in our interconnected world, making it easy for Stoicism to gain popularity rapidly.

Universal Appeal: Stoicism resonates with people because everyone desires strength, resilience, self-confidence, and control over their lives. Stoicism offers a straightforward recipe for achieving these goals.

Abundance of Resources: Numerous books and websites dedicated to Stoicism and modern interpretations are published each year. Examples include Ward Farnsworth's "The Stoic Practitioner" and websites like Re-Made-Stoicism, making ancient philosophy easily accessible.

Social Institutions Breakdown: Traditional institutions like churches, schools, and family structures, which once provided a sense of purpose, are now often broken or less influential. With the rise of the digital world, people seek stability in the timeless teachings of Stoicism amidst a rapidly changing society.

Universality of Wisdom: Stoic advice is timeless and universally applicable. It focuses on understanding human nature, dealing with both others and oneself, and navigating the complexities of life. This universality makes Stoicism a philosophy for all times.

Why Explore Stoic Philosophy?

Let's be honest—life can be challenging. It doesn't always go the way we want, and it often feels like we're facing constant setbacks. The Stoics had a unique perspective on dealing with life's uncertainties, focusing on building a strong internal control center.

This internal control means taking responsibility for your success or failure in this world. Forget using your past as an excuse for being passive or feeling like a victim. The Stoic approach is straightforward: "So, what are you going to do about it?" How will you respond to today's challenges?

Starting from ground zero, the Stoics believed they had enough motivation, strength, and determination to adapt to life's conditions and thrive. They emphasized that each individual is responsible for their actions and the energy they bring to various interactions. To strengthen their internal control, Stoics focused on three key areas, starting with:

External Factors:

The Stoics acknowledged that what we admire and where we invest our energy are external aspects. They questioned why anyone would be surprised if they felt dread and anguish, given their focus on external circumstances like time, politics, other people's actions, job loss, illness, or even death itself. To navigate these external challenges, the Stoics recommended self-discipline, mindfulness, and creating emotional distance—a philosophy similar to Buddhism.

The Stoic would prefer sunny weather, harmonious politics, good health, and life going smoothly. However, they are not overly concerned about whether these external conditions align with their preferences. They embody the "independence of the result" philosophy, taking a proactive approach to life by asking: "What is the next best action, and where do we go from here?" It's a powerful mindset shift from self-pity to regaining control over one's actions.

Death

Seneca advises, "Whatever you do, think about death." Death is an inevitable part of life, and Stoics view it with intense consideration, making it a central theme in their philosophy. In works like "On the Shortness of Life," Seneca suggests that it takes a lifetime to learn not only how to live but also how to face death.

Learning to live fully requires an awareness of our mortality, but many people fear death, leading them to overlook the vitality of their lives. Stoics caution against measuring a good life solely by its length, as it's a mindset that hinders personal growth and the improvement of one's actions.

In modern Stoicism, death is emphasized as something relevant to everyone. Rather than treating it as an abstract concept happening to others, Stoics encourage living each day purposefully. It's easy to spend a lifetime unaware of the preciousness of time, emphasizing the need to pay attention to every moment and infuse our actions with purpose as if each day were our last on earth.

Equanimity (Tranquility):

Stoics seek spiritual presence and peace of mind in all life circumstances, even when facing overwhelming fear. The primary goal is to strengthen the will through adversity, akin to adding logs to a fire.

Epictetus compares the Stoic approach to "Hermes' wand," suggesting that challenges can be transformed into valuable experiences. Regardless of life's adversities—disease, death, poverty, insults, or high crimes—Stoicism aims to turn these challenges into opportunities for growth.

The Stoic pursuit is not to be overwhelmed by the emotional turbulence and dramas of modern life. Instead, it aims to maintain a balanced mental state capable of turning challenging situations into neutral or even positive ones. Achieving this requires concentration and pragmatism—qualities that propel individuals toward their goals efficiently.

Living Modern Stoic Philosophy:

Modern Stoicism isn't just about studying—it's a philosophy meant to be lived and practiced in your daily life. Here are some practical ways to embrace the Stoic mindset:

Aim for Virtue:

The core of Stoicism is living a virtuous life—being of service, showing compassion, and practicing goodwill towards others. To achieve virtue, you must embody the highest good in yourself, regardless of the situation. Ask yourself, "What would my best self do?" or draw inspiration from examples. This provides guidance in navigating ambiguous situations.

Focus on Continuous Improvement:

Stoicism is a way of thinking and living that revolves around constant improvement. The Stoics were keen on adapting, even to things once deemed challenging. Seneca's words, "Nothing is so difficult that the human mind cannot conquer it and make it familiar through constant practice," highlight the Stoic emphasis on continuous learning. Plan ways to improve from yesterday and actively follow through with that plan.

Learn to Live with Others:

Life doesn't happen in isolation; it involves interactions with other people. The Stoics emphasized engagement in civil service and living among others while maintaining a higher perspective. Marcus Aurelius, in his meditations, acknowledges that people can be involved, ungrateful, arrogant, dishonest, jealous, and grumpy. However, understanding their nature and shared humanity can help in navigating interactions more effectively. The Stoic lifestyle is ultimately centered around people.

Stoicism offers a framework for a more harmonious and productive life. By studying and applying Stoic principles, you can navigate life's challenges without being discouraged, making the most of the limited time we have. The goal is not just understanding Stoicism intellectually but actively integrating its teachings into your daily experiences for a more fulfilling life.

CHAPTER 6:
FOUNDATIONS OF
STOIC PHILOSOPHY

The Basis of Stoic Force

In Stoicism, there's a lesson so crucial that Mariano, a student of Epictetus, puts it in the first three sentences of Enchiridion. If you grasp this teaching and commit to the stoic mindset, it becomes a powerful source of invincibility. However, if you overlook this lesson, the entire philosophy might seem meaningless. Consistently applying this simple truth in every moment of choice, according to Mariano, turns you into an unbeatable athlete.

Some Background

Enchiridion, a concise compilation of Stoic teachings, is based on Epictetus's statements. Originally from eight books, only four have survived over time. Half of the chapters in the current books come from the surviving ones, while the other half are from the lost books. The term "enchiridion" means "handbook" in ancient Greek, and philosophy students use these guides to support their practice when away from their teacher.

The First Lesson

This short manual begins by introducing the concept of the "control dichotomy." Enchiridion 1 states:

"A few things are in our capacity, and a few things are past our capacity."

At first glance, it may not seem like profound wisdom, but the essence lies in understanding what falls within our control. It lists items within our control as opinion, goal, desire, aversion, and, in essence, everything that is ours.

The dichotomy becomes even more interesting when it delves into what lies beyond our control. It includes the body, possessions, reputation, position, and, in a nutshell, everything that isn't our concern.

Challenging Modern Perceptions

At this point, modern sensibilities may raise objections. People often claim, "I may not have full control over my body, but I can manage it to some extent through a healthy lifestyle." Similar sentiments are expressed about reputation and income.

However, the Stoic perspective is clear—there is no "partial control." The dichotomy is binary, a stark distinction between what we can control and what we cannot. It's either a check or no check, on or off. Understanding and accepting this concept is fundamental to unlocking the true power of Stoicism.

Partial control over our moods involves making decisions about certain behaviors. We can choose to eat well, engage in sports, and ensure we get adequate rest. However, this doesn't imply control over our health; rather, we influence it through our decisions. Influence doesn't equate to control; it's not even a partial form of control. Our decisions aim to achieve specific results, but the outcomes are not within our control. We make decisions, and events unfold as they may.

Our bodies react to stimuli based on our choices or by chance. When we cut ourselves, the body heals; when exposed to the sun, it sweats. Eating, chewing, and swallowing food lead to digestion, and lifting weights regularly develops muscle tissue. All these processes occur naturally, barring organic problems like diseases or hormonal imbalances.

Let's not delve into examples related to reputation or wealth; it's evident. The body is initially listed as beyond our control, challenging any claims of control over external factors. However, this perspective doesn't dismiss external control claims entirely.

Consider if everything is either within our control or beyond it—or if some things are within our control while others are in the control of external forces. For instance, if you had the perfect body, is it within your control? No, it's not. Health, beauty, the timing of living or dying—all beyond our control. The body is subject to forces stronger than itself.

Further exploration includes scenarios where someone might impede your progress. Can any part of you hold back? No, your body acts like a stone, limiting your movement. Even your hand, while part of you, tends to resist and is influenced by forces stronger than itself.

The use of our bodies and anything requiring their assistance is not within our control. Despite having a goal, desire, and intention to achieve an external result, we cannot guarantee it. Even if the achievement depends on something as basic as taking a breath, we can only aim to breathe; the actual act is subject to fate.

What Remains?

In the Stoic philosophy of Epictetus, our power is so limited that even our bodies lack command over us. If we can't rely on the body's ability to take a breath at any given moment, what do we have left?

Amidst all our limitations, there's one thing we confront: our prohairesis. In ancient Greek, prohairesis translates to "choice," "will," "intention," or "preparation." Epictetus viewed our prohairesis as the essence of ourselves—the sole power we possess. It is not only the only power but also the only force necessary.

Before delving into strategies for making good use of our choices, it's crucial to understand why accepting such a limited perspective is essential in transforming into what I term an athlete of stoic strength.

CHAPTER 7: ANGER AND STOICISM

Anger, according to the Stoics, is like a passing state of madness that they have learned to control. People can become angry for various reasons, ranging from minor inconveniences like someone cutting them off on the highway to more significant issues, such as the ongoing suffering of the Syrian people with no resolution in sight. Interestingly, many problems that lead to anger often stem from trivial causes.

Recognizing the prevalence of anger-related issues, the American Psychological Association has dedicated a section on its website to anger management. It's intriguing to note that this modern approach aligns with the wisdom found in one of the oldest texts on the subject—On Anger—penned by the Stoic philosopher Lucius Annaeus Seneca in the first century AD.

Seneca's perspective on anger is insightful. He viewed anger as a temporary form of madness and advised against acting on it, even if it seemed justified. Seneca argued that, unlike other vices that subtly influence our judgment, anger directly impacts our mental well-being. It can make us easily attack others while our rational thoughts get submerged in a sudden burst of rage. What's interesting is that the intensity of anger doesn't necessarily correlate with its origin; even the most trivial incidents can lead to extreme outbursts. This Stoic insight provides valuable guidance on how to approach and manage anger in our lives.

The Internet has become an ideal space for exploring the principles of anger management, especially with the prevalence of platforms like Twitter, Facebook, blogs, and online discussions. Interactions with people globally are generally warm and instructive, but occasionally, things take an unpleasant turn. In a recent encounter, a well-known author disagreed with me on a technical issue and resorted to name-calling, labeling me a member of a "bad department." It stings, especially when such comments come from someone famous with a massive following of over 500,000 people. Following the advice of Stoic philosopher Epictetus, who taught his students to recognize that we are the ones who create problems for ourselves, becomes crucial. He encouraged adopting a resilient mindset, comparing it to standing firm like a stone against ridicule. Epictetus questioned the effectiveness of contemptuous remarks when met with a response resembling a stone's indifference.

Developing a stoic attitude towards insults takes time and practice, but progress is achievable. In response to the mentioned abuse, I chose to act like a stone. Instead of dwelling on the insult, I redirected my energy toward addressing genuine questions from others and fostering effective relationships. Interestingly, this approach seemed to leave the famous writer frustrated, as they were met with silence rather than a reciprocal outburst of anger.

Some argue that anger can be an appropriate response to certain situations, such as in the face of injustice, and may, in moderation, serve as a motivating force for action. However, Seneca, the Stoic philosopher, would counter that moderate anger is as rare as flying pigs—something nonexistent in the universe. From a stoic perspective, motivation to act should stem from positive emotions like a sense of indignation, witnessing injustice, or a desire to contribute to a better world. Anger, according to Stoicism, is deemed unnecessary and usually falls in the realm of excess.

Martha Nussbaum, a renowned philosopher, shared a contemporary example in her essay about Nelson Mandela. Despite enduring 27 years of imprisonment under the South African apartheid government, Mandela initially harbored intense anger due to the injustice not only against him but also against his people. However, Mandela realized that nurturing this anger and viewing his political opponents as inhuman would hinder progress. To bring about positive change, he needed to overcome destructive emotions, build trust, and even form friendships. A crucial influence on Mandela's transformation was a Stoic philosophy book, Marcus Aurelius' Meditations, smuggled to him by a fellow inmate. This Stoic philosophy emphasized teaching and showing without anger when addressing wrongs, a principle Mandela effectively applied in his journey.

Drawing inspiration from Seneca's advice, here's a modern guide to stoic anger management:

- Meditate beforehand: Reflect on situations that trigger anger and decide how to respond.
- Check anger symptoms immediately; don't let it escalate out of control.
- Engage with calm individuals, avoiding those in an agitated state, as moods are contagious.
- Play a musical instrument or engage in activities that relax your mind to prevent anger.
- Seek environments with pleasant colors, as external circumstances impact mood.
- Avoid engaging in discussions when tired, as fatigue can lead to irritability and anger.
- Similarly, refrain from starting discussions when thirsty or hungry.

- Utilize self-deprecating humor as a defense against life's unpredictability and human wickedness.
- Practice cognitive distancing by delaying reactions — take a walk or step away during tense situations.
- Change your body language intentionally, adopting the calm demeanor of a relaxed person.
- Embrace charity as a pathway to a good life, aligning with Seneca's successful anger management advice. Following these principles can contribute to a more balanced and fulfilling life.

A Stoic Reaction to Anger

"Keep this thought in mind when anger strikes – it is not a sign of true strength to be angry. Kindness and compassion are more human and, therefore, more powerful. A genuine person, whether male or female, exhibits strength, courage, and resilience – qualities that stand in contrast to anger and complaints. The closer one gets to a calm mind, the closer they are to real strength." - Marcus Aurelius.

There are moments in life when things go awry. Someone might be impolite, your car could break down, or an employee might mess up despite clear instructions. Your instinct may push you towards anger – a natural reaction.

However, just because it's a natural reaction doesn't make it a wise one. Recall Marcus Aurelius' insight:

"How much more harmful are the consequences of anger... compared to the circumstances that provoked us."

Yelling might provide temporary relief, but does it truly solve the problem? Arguing with a rude person often only encourages further rudeness. If you're angry about car troubles, your car won't miraculously repair itself, and your blood pressure will only rise. Insulting an employee who made a mistake? They may resent you or perform worse in the future due to nerves and lack of confidence.

In his essay on anger, Seneca advises,

"The best plan is to immediately reject the initial triggers for anger, resist its beginnings, and be cautious not to betray ourselves. Once the passion takes hold of the mind and gains authority through our free will, it will act as it pleases in the future, not just within the limits you allow. Find and restrain the enemy early, as once it gains entry and breaches the gates, it won't let prisoners set boundaries on its victory."

Your emotions are a choice: choose anger over peace; choose fear instead of courage; choose misery over joy. Which choice is more productive? What does anger punish, and what impact do circumstances truly have? Remember, circumstances remain unchanged because you're upset with them. After all, circumstances aren't people.

Avoid wasting your time and energy on things that are completely indifferent to your emotions. Cease believing that emotions can alter the nature of lifeless objects, situations, or entities. It's akin to ingesting poison and expecting someone else to suffer its effects.

Emotions contribute nothing constructive. In fact, anger only worsens the situation. A fresh and composed mind is key to navigating challenges. Even individuals who recognize anger as a potent and impactful tool will emphasize the significant difference between expressing pain constructively (to make a point or encourage someone to defend themselves) and allowing it to explode uncontrollably. Failing to identify and control your emotions means becoming enslaved by them.

If Stoicism imparts only one lesson, even if you disregard all other valuable teachings, this alone is sufficient to test and transform you throughout your life. It holds enough value to bring about lifelong change.

5 Ways to Deal with Stoicism

The most famous follower of Stoicism was the Roman emperor Marcus Aurelius, who passed away in 180 AD. His personal journal filled with philosophical reflections, "Meditations," stands as one of the most widely read spiritual works and self-help essays. Within its pages are numerous instances of the mental exercises the emperor employed to maintain his inner equilibrium during the Marcomannic Wars fought along the Danube against invading tribes.

Marcus Aurelius is renowned for his struggle to master his anger. Throughout his book, he revisits this theme, recalling various ideas that proved beneficial in combating anger. At one point, he outlined ten practical strategies for anger management, which he dubbed "the gifts of Apollo," the god of healing. Here are five:

#1 Strategy: Acknowledge Your Imperfections

Stoics emphasized the importance of recognizing our own flaws. When you find yourself offended by someone, pause and reflect on whether you could engage in similar behavior or possess the potential to do things that might be offensive to others. In essence, as therapists suggest, notice the three fingers of the same hand pointing back at you when pointing out someone else's guilt. Acknowledging our capability to commit similar wrongs can often lessen our anger and provide a more rational perspective on the situation.

#2 Strategy: It's Your Judgment, Not the Behavior, That Provokes You

This fundamental Stoic principle and psychological strategy prompt self-reflection. Do you consistently feel equally annoyed by the same behavior in various contexts or when performed by different people? Different reactions among individuals may arise from diverse attitudes and opinions about the situation. According to Stoicism, our value judgments determine the intensity of our anger toward life events. It's worthwhile to consider this perspective and question whether we assign too much importance to things beyond our direct influence.

#3 Strategy: Your Anger Harms You More Than the Source of Your Anger

Another prevalent Stoic teaching emphasizes that anger not only distorts our facial expressions but also clouds our reasoning ability. Stoics describe anger as a temporary madness. While the actions of others may harm external aspects like possessions, reputation, or physical well-being, according to Stoicism, succumbing to anger further damages our moral character. Deliberately reflecting on the potential negative consequences of yielding to anger can often help mitigate its impact on our mental well-being.

#4 Strategy: Consider the Possibility of Misunderstanding

Socrates imparted the surprising yet contentious teaching that no one knowingly commits evil. Marcus Aurelius observed that individuals often defend their actions when confronted. Even when accused of moral wrongdoing, people tend to justify their behavior. Even notorious figures like Hitler and Stalin believed their actions were justified. Criminals, aware of the illegality of their deeds, still find ways to rationalize their actions. Ancient philosophers engaged in thorough ethical discussions with ordinary people, understanding how individuals often feign knowledge of right and wrong. Marcus advises acknowledging the inherent confusion in people's lives to temper one's anger.

#5 Strategy: Rise Above Anger; Respond with Compassion

Stoics not only confronted their own anger but also advocated for a more compassionate perspective. Stoicism embodies a philosophy rooted in compassion. According to Stoics, anger typically stems from the belief that someone has committed a wrong and deserves punishment. The alternative perspective involves believing that individuals should be assisted or uplifted. Marcus Aurelius expressed that if confronted with someone's hostile behavior, he would, after addressing his own anger, kindly approach the person and explain without condescension, emphasizing that their actions harmed themselves more than anyone else.

Sixteen Best Ways to Outsmart Anger

The ancient Stoics were aware of the destructive nature of anger. Seneca, for instance, regarded it as a scourge that has inflicted great harm on humanity. While expressing anger might give us a momentary sense of satisfaction, most people dislike being angry and prefer not to be around those who are angry. Generally, anger tends to worsen situations rather than improve them. As the Buddha aptly put it, "Giving up anger is like drinking poison and waiting for the person to die."

So, how can we steer clear of anger? Here are 16 ways based on the teachings of the ancient Stoics, primarily from Marcus Aurelius, Seneca, and Epictetus:

#1 Recognize That It's Your Perception Causing Anger

Often, we believe that someone else's actions provoke our anger. In reality, it's our interpretation of their actions that triggers anger. For example, if someone calls you an idiot, instead of reacting angrily, you can choose to ignore it, recognizing that it's merely their opinion.

#2 Understand the Consequences of Anger

While the initial surge of anger may feel empowering, it's crucial to recognize that anger carries consequences. It can harm your reputation and have legal, moral, or material repercussions. Before expressing anger, take a moment to consider the potential consequences.

#3 Acknowledge That Your Anger Harms You More Than The Cause

Reflect on the true cost of anger. Even if you believe your anger is justified, consider that the toll it takes on your well-being far outweighs the satisfaction gained. Anger amplifies the damage caused by the initial triggering event.

#4 Acknowledge the Commonality Between You and The Person Who Annoys You

When irritation arises towards someone, consider the shared humanity that binds us. As humans, our actions often stem from similar desires. While one person may believe happiness lies in accumulating wealth, another may find it in helping others. Why harbor anger towards someone who pursues happiness in a different way?

#5 Reflect on Moments When You've Engaged in Similar Actions

In instances of anger, it's common to overlook our own past behaviors that mirror those of the person causing irritation. Taking a retrospective look may reveal that we've acted similarly in the past, even though we justified our actions without extending the same understanding to others.

#6 Recognize That the Consequences of Others' Wrongs are not Yours to Bear

Allow others to face the repercussions of their actions. By getting angry, you end up burdened with the consequences of your anger, while the responsibility for their actions remains with them.

#7 Acknowledge the Ignorance of the Other Person

Deliberate harm from someone often stems from ignorance. Instead of responding with anger, offer understanding or pity. Recognize that an ignorant person is in need of enlightenment rather than your wrath.

#8 Realize That Your Anger Goes Against the Natural Order

Anger is inherently oppositional, pitting one person against another. However, just as different bodily organs function together, we are interconnected. If you experience pain, you don't direct anger at the affected body part; similarly, when someone wrongs you, there's no need for animosity. We are all integral parts of the same whole, and hostility contradicts our natural unity.

#9 Acknowledge That Your Anger May Be Unfair

Justice demands accurate judgment based on all available facts. Anger typically arises without a full understanding of the situation, responding to hasty "impressions" rather than a thorough examination of the facts. Someone seemingly ignoring a farewell may have underlying health issues, and a person overlooking your kindness might be shy rather than intentionally hostile.

#10 Acknowledge That Your Anger May Stem From Misperceptions

Frequently, anger arises from a sense of entitlement or perceived justification. Feeling angry when someone ignores us may be rooted in a belief that we deserve respect. Being upset with the government may arise from the notion that we are entitled to pay fewer taxes. Eliminate anger by recognizing that entitlements are often unfounded, and we have no inherent right to external circumstances.

#11 Realize Your Capacity to Resist

Anger often arises when we feel overwhelmed. However, you possess internal resources such as perseverance and patience to navigate situations without succumbing to anger. Acknowledge your inner strength, avoid helplessness, and resist being swayed by others' actions or your anger.

#12 Understand That Others' Actions are Beyond Your Control, but Your Reactions are Within Your Control

While someone's words may provoke anger, the decision to get angry is within your control. Focus on what you can manage – your emotional response. Trying to control external events is futile; instead, redirect your energy towards mastering your reactions.

#13 Realize That Situations Have Alternative Perspectives

In moments of anger, it may seem that anger is the only appropriate response. Challenge this notion by recognizing there are alternative ways to handle a situation. For instance, if a friend's comment upsets you, consider an alternative perspective: "He's been a good friend, and while his words hurt, I've hurt others too." This shift in perspective can dissipate anger.

#14 Understand The Brevity of Life

Contemplate the shortness of life, realizing that both you and the source of your anger are transient. Adopt a broader perspective; ask yourself if it's worth squandering life in a fleeting moment of anger.

#15 Avoid People and Situations That Escalate Your Anger

While not a comprehensive solution, minimizing exposure to individuals and circumstances that trigger your anger can be a practical step. However, the ultimate goal is to eliminate anger altogether, not merely sidestep its immediate causes.

#16 Cultivate a Contrasting Mindset

Break the cycle of anger, which can become habitual, by adopting a contrary attitude. Laughter serves as an opposing habit since it is challenging to be simultaneously angry and amused. When anger arises, find humor in the situation, smile, or laugh at the intensity of your expression.

Stoic Perspectives and Approaches to Anger

Many of us find it easy to get angry with people we interact with regularly, like family, friends, colleagues, or neighbors. Feeling offended or upset when others don't meet our expectations is a common experience.

When we get annoyed by someone (or even by things), we usually believe they've done something to harm or inconvenience us. But just feeling hurt isn't enough to justify anger. We also need to see their actions as unfair or unjust.

Anger involves not just feeling hurt, but also wanting to retaliate against the person who hurt us. Stoics believe anger is always harmful. They're firm about this, even though other philosophies might see it differently.

Marcus Aurelius, a famous Stoic philosopher, once seemed to make an exception. He agreed with a philosopher named Theophrastus that actions done out of anger might be less bad than those driven by desires for pleasure. However, even in these cases, violence is still wrong, just not as bad as some other harmful actions.

Why is anger such a big deal, and why is it considered "bad"? Seneca, in her writings on violence, talks about how anger can make a person's face look twisted, ugly, and scary. This change in appearance, which can be noticed and controlled through techniques like the "eye to eye" method, is just one small part of the problem with anger. When someone is angry, their distorted appearance, posture, and voice reveal deeper issues within them.

Epictetus, in agreement with Seneca, points out that we often focus on physical or material losses as injuries, but we ignore the harm done to our moral character. Our moral purpose, or ability to make choices, is damaged when we give in to anger.

When we act on anger, we usually want to retaliate or hurt the person who made us angry, even if it's just imagined retaliation like muttering insults under our breath. Sometimes, this retaliation can actually harm the other person. While Stoics might debate whether the person is truly harmed or just perceives harm, most people, including ourselves, will feel hurt by angry outbursts, silent treatment, or other expressions of anger.

Anger not only hurts others but also damages ourselves, which is a serious problem. This is why Epictetus highlights the irrationality of anger. For example, if a friend repeatedly cancels plans with us to spend time with others and shares photos of their fun on social media, it's natural to feel hurt and maybe even angry. However,

Stoic philosophy suggests that we shouldn't interpret this as a personal attack and instead focus on understanding the situation without letting anger cloud our judgment.

Picture this: I'm really angry, and it feels like the right thing to do is to get back at the person who upset me. Maybe I'm hot-headed, so I call my friend and leave a mean message on their voicemail. Or I gossip about them behind their back. Or, in a really risky move, I confront them at a party and things escalate into a physical fight.

All of these actions are driven by my anger, and they can cause the other person a lot of emotional pain. There might also be "collateral damage," like other people feeling anxious, scared, disgusted, or even joyful, depending on how they see the situation.

Anger doesn't just harm others; it hurts me too, both in the short term and in the long run. It makes me let go of the good qualities I've built in myself. Stoic philosophy offers different ways to think about this loss. One way is through the concept of virtue, or being a good person. Another is by considering the damage to my own character. When I give in to anger, it's like I'm causing a real wound to myself, even though it might not seem that way at first.

There's a tricky way of thinking that kicks in when I'm angry, and if I'm not careful, I'll follow it without even realizing. This way of thinking feels totally logical and necessary in the moment, but it's actually irrational and harmful, as Stoic thinkers like Epictetus point out. Unless we consciously recognize and challenge this harmful thinking, we might not see how damaging anger can be for us in the long term.

Another Way We Can Change Our Face

The Stoics aren't just a group focused solely on studying anger; they're also deeply interested in understanding violence and how it impacts us. They teach us to examine our perceptions and traditions, guiding us towards a path where we become less prone to anger and gain better control over our emotions, find greater purpose, and achieve more inner harmony.

Their discussions with their intellectual rivals, the Aristotelians and Epicureans, provide valuable insights. However, the Stoics, drawing from ancient texts, offer us advanced strategies for changing our perspectives and emotional responses, particularly regarding anger. These strategies extend beyond violence and touch on various aspects of our lives, including reasoning, beliefs, emotions, desires, dislikes, and decision-making.

One powerful method they advocate, emphasized by Epictetus, is distinguishing between what we can control and what we cannot. This concept, outlined in the Enchiridion, holds a central place in Stoic philosophy. While Epictetus elaborates on this distinction further in his speeches, there are two crucial points to understand.

Firstly, many people, including ourselves and our societies, often misunderstand this differentiation. It takes continuous practice, discipline, and reflection to grasp it fully. We must remind ourselves regularly of what falls within our control and what does not.

Secondly, this differentiation overlaps with another critical aspect of Stoic moral theory: distinguishing between what is truly good or bad in itself and what is indifferent. Understanding this helps prevent us from assigning undue importance to things beyond our control, which can lead us to confuse what is truly beneficial or harmful for us.

Understanding some implications isn't too tricky; we can pick the low-hanging fruits of wisdom. Many of the things that bug us are actually beyond our control and don't really matter. When we misunderstand these things, it can lead to all sorts of problems—disappointment, frustration, and even anger—instead of other emotions like sadness or fear.

When we get angry, it's because we feel hurt and want to get even or feel justified, even if it's only partially true. This desire for revenge or justice makes anger more complicated.

Anger often stems from misunderstanding what we can and can't control. It also tricks us into thinking we have control over things we don't—like expecting the person who angered us to react a certain way or how others will perceive our anger. Meanwhile, things we actually can control, like our own reactions, seem beyond our grasp, shifting the blame onto others. For example, saying, "They made me lose control," is a common way to deflect responsibility.

Similarly, misunderstandings about what's truly good or bad aren't just limited to anger; anger actually worsens this confusion. Seneca's "On Anger" elaborates on this point eloquently. When we're angry, we not only overlook the actual value of things like reason, our shared humanity, and truth itself, but we also mistakenly view seeking revenge as something desirable. This desire seems to align with our inner feelings, desires, and judgments, making it appear more important than anything else in the situation.

While it's not easy, with practice, we can change our habits and remember these crucial differences in Stoic philosophy when we feel or experience anger.

Imagine going to a crowded public bathhouse. People might splash water on you, push you around, or even steal from you. To stay calm in such situations, remind yourself that your primary goal is to bathe while maintaining your moral integrity. If something disrupts your bath, acknowledge that while cleanliness was your initial aim, preserving your moral intentions is equally important. Getting angry won't achieve this.

As discussed throughout this book, prioritizing moral integrity in harmony with nature may seem abstract, but there are concrete ways to remind ourselves of it.

Another important implication of these distinctions is that we can't control others' actions; that's their responsibility. How they behave depends on their perspective, which may differ from ours. While their actions may seem frustrating or even harmful, it's they who suffer the consequences, not us.

Marcus Aurelius offers a helpful perspective on dealing with actions of others that might annoy us. He suggests that when someone hurts us, we should consider what consequences, both good and bad, would follow. By understanding this, we're more likely to feel empathy rather than anger. Our understanding of right and wrong might align with theirs, leading to forgiveness. Or it might differ, in which case we should recognize our own misunderstanding and offer ourselves compassion. This isn't easy.

Epictetus and Seneca echo this advice. Another valuable suggestion, mentioned by various authors, is to imagine ourselves in the other person's shoes. Seneca advises us to consider how our inflated sense of importance often fuels our anger, leading us to do things we wouldn't want done to us.

While it's simpler to sympathize with others' struggles than to apply this to our own experiences, it's something we should strive for. That's why it's important to focus on understanding what's within the "will of nature," rather than fixating on our differences.

An Important Consideration: What Happens if You Let Go of Anger?

As we conclude our discussion, I'd like to address another topic that we touched upon in the book but didn't delve into deeply. Many people who struggle with anger often wonder what life would be like without it. Making a conscious decision to move away from anger as a go-to emotional response raises concerns about how to navigate situations without it. Speaking from experience, choosing to let go of anger, especially when faced with wrongdoing, can feel like disarming yourself in the midst of conflict, leaving you vulnerable.

This concern is valid to some extent. If a person has relied on anger as their primary means of handling various situations successfully (or so it seemed), they'll likely feel disadvantaged at first. Anger isn't just a sporadic emotion—it becomes ingrained in habits and rooted in other human behaviors.

For instance, if a child learns early on that angry outbursts help resolve conflicts and correct perceived wrongs, possibly by observing parental behavior, by the time they're an adult, anger becomes a default reaction. Breaking this habit and replacing it with new ones feels unnatural and uncomfortable, leaving the person unsure of how to cope.

In Seneca's work on anger, he challenges common perceptions of anger as noble, necessary, or useful. He acknowledges that these views, influenced by Aristotelian and classical cultural beliefs, may initially seem plausible. However, upon closer examination, their irrationality becomes evident.

Aristotle suggests that certain emotions, when used correctly, can be like weapons. However, unlike physical weapons that can be wielded or set aside at will, these emotional "weapons" of virtue operate independently. They don't wait for us to control them; instead, they control us.

This presents a significant problem. When anger is not under control, it not only fails to serve its intended purpose but also inhibits the proper functioning and development of human rationality, as Seneca highlights.

So, what could be more foolish than seeking protection from reason itself? Reason is inherently more powerful, even when it comes to tasks that might seem to require the aid of anger. When reason decides on a course of action, it remains steadfast. Those struggling with anger should remember that, although it may initially seem otherwise, reason provides a much safer path for human conduct, protecting us from harm. A Stoic life is one that continually seeks rationality, even if complete freedom from anger may not be attainable for many of us. Nonetheless, reason allows us to effectively manage anger when it arises.

CHAPTER 8: PEACE OF MIND

The image of a Zen scientist often conjures up visions of a peaceful monk in a serene environment like a green landscape or a beautiful temple. However, Stoicism presents a different scene. It's not about retreating to secluded places but about thriving in the hustle and bustle of everyday life.

Stoicism is about finding tranquility and clarity amidst the chaos of the market, the streets, the council chambers, or even the battlefield. In essence, Stoics are just like you and me.

Although these settings may not seem conducive to philosophical contemplation, they are. Stoicism has been practiced by people from all walks of life for thousands of years, from slaves to emperors, in their pursuit of wisdom, power, and a good life. It's a practical philosophy for everyone, not just for a specific class.

That's why Stoicism has resonated with figures like Marcus Aurelius and Seneca, who were influential in ancient Rome, as well as with modern figures like Theodore Roosevelt, Frederick the Great, and Michel de Montaigne.

How can we emulate the timeless wisdom of the Stoics in our daily lives, especially in the workplace? It's simple: turn to the original teachings. Below, you'll find practical Stoic exercises and strategies that can assist you in navigating your professional environment with clarity, efficiency, and serenity.

#1 Don't Overcomplicate Things

Imagine someone asking you how to write your name. Would you shout out every letter? And if they got angry, would you react with anger too? Wouldn't it be better to calmly spell out each letter for them? Marcus Aurelius reminds us that our duties in life are made up of every action we take. So, when facing tasks, keep this in mind.

Here's a common scenario: You're dealing with a difficult colleague or a demanding boss. They ask you to do something, and if you don't like them, you immediately reject their request. Maybe their approach is rude or unpleasant. So, you refuse, saying, "No, I won't do it." Then, they retaliate by not doing what you've asked them to do before. And so, the conflict escalates.

But if you step back and look at the situation objectively, you might realize that not everything asked of you is unreasonable. In fact, some parts might be quite manageable or even enjoyable. By doing those first, you might find the rest of the task more bearable. It's about taking simple and appropriate actions on the path of virtue, without letting emotions get in the way.

#2 Impossible Without Your Consent

Today, I managed to detach myself from being overwhelmed by circumstances. These feelings didn't come from outside but from within me.

During tough times, we might say, "My job is too demanding," or "My boss is always upset." But if we understand that external circumstances cannot control us unless we allow them to, we regain power over our emotions. Stoics use the term "hypolepsis," meaning to welcome or accept, to explain that what we perceive, think, and judge depends on us. We can't blame others for our stress or envy; it's within ourselves. We are in control of our reactions.

#3 A Positive Mindset

"Here's a way to organize your thoughts: remind yourself that you're not controlled by your past, you're not swayed by every impulse like a puppet, and you won't dwell on current possessions or worry about the future." - Marcus Aurelius

We often get irritated when someone tries to dictate how we should live. We proclaim our independence and self-sufficiency, but deep down, we still feel compelled to argue when faced with disagreement or indulge in every impulse, good or bad.

We wouldn't tolerate someone else controlling us like we do with our own impulses. It's time to recognize that we're not puppets; we should be the ones in control of our actions, not our impulses.

#4 Keep It Simple

"Approach every task with discipline, simplicity, dignity, affection, freedom, and justice—free from distractions, emotional upheavals, drama, vanity, and complaints." - Marcus Aurelius

Each day presents us with choices: what to wear, what to eat, what lies ahead. But let's focus solely on the present. Like the New

England Patriots coach advises his players: "Do your job." Avoid getting distracted by others' activities or countless other concerns.

Marcus suggests treating every task as if it were your last, striving for perfection even if it's not achievable. Find clarity and fulfillment in the simplicity of focused action.

#5 Never Act Out Of Habit

"In most cases, we don't respond to situations with the right mindset, but rather out of habit. Therefore, those who strive to improve themselves must work to break free from seeking pleasure and avoiding pain, from clinging to life and fearing death, and from valuing receiving over giving." -
Musonius Rufus

Consider this scenario: an officer questions an employee's method, and the response is, "Because that's how we've always done it." This habitual response frustrates good leadership and invites competition. It's a sign that the worker is functioning on autopilot, which can lead to dismissal under a discerning boss.

We should approach our habits with a similar critical eye. Philosophy teaches us to break free from unproductive behaviors. Examine what you do out of habit. Ask yourself if it's truly the best approach and if you're acting for the right reasons.

#6 Your Career Shouldn't Define You

"How shameful is the lawyer whose last breath is spent arguing in court, chasing cases, and seeking validation from ignorant onlookers." - Seneca

We often witness a sad spectacle: an elderly mogul embroiled in legal battles over their business empire. Their failure to delegate or plan for succession leads to public exposure of their vulnerabilities. We shouldn't let our work consume us to the point where we're blind to the realities of aging and life. Do you want to be the person who can't let go, whose life revolves solely around work?

Take pride in your work, but remember, it's not your entire life.

#7 Protect Your Peace

"Always monitor your perceptions, for it's not external events that disturb you, but your judgment of them, your reliance on them, your tranquility, your freedom from pain and fear. What price would you pay to preserve these?" - *Epictetus*

Stoicism helps us control our emotional reactions, allowing us to navigate challenging situations with ease. But consider: why subject yourself to environments that constantly provoke stress? Are the endless work problems truly worth sacrificing your peace of mind? Redirect your focus towards what truly matters in life. Don't be afraid to make significant changes for your well-being.

CHAPTER 9: STOIC WAYS TO USE SILENCE EFFECTIVELY

In August 1919, the famous psychologist Milton Erickson got a serious illness called poliomyelitis, which was quite common back then. Milton was just 17 when his doctor said he might not make it through the night. But as the days turned into weeks, and he found himself unable to move except for his eyes, Milton didn't let himself feel sorry for himself. Instead, he became intensely curious about the world around him.

One day, while listening to his sisters talking, Milton noticed something interesting. Even though one of them said, "This is a great idea" with a smile, her voice sounded dull. Milton realized that her words didn't match her true feelings. He began studying people's facial expressions and emotions, using his enforced silence as a way to learn about human nature.

This story, taken from Robert Greene's book about human behavior, shows us something important: we often miss a lot in our conversations because we're not paying enough attention. Sometimes we talk too much about ourselves, or we don't listen well enough to others.

The ancient Stoics, like Zeno, Marcus Aurelius, Seneca, and Epictetus, understood the power of words. They wrote about the importance of speaking thoughtfully and being mindful of how our words can hurt others.

Here are the suggestions from our beloved Stoics on accomplishing more with fewer words.

Listen Up: The Power of Silence in Helping Others

Have you ever felt the urge to jump in and solve someone's problem the moment they open up to you? It's natural to want to help, but sometimes the best help we can offer is simply to listen.

Think about it this way: we're born with two ears and one mouth for a reason – to listen twice as much as we speak. Yet, when someone pours their heart out to us, we often rush to analyze and advise them. We may mean well, but in doing so, we miss the true purpose of their sharing – they just need a listening ear.

Stoic philosophy teaches us the importance of active listening. Instead of rushing to give advice, we should focus on truly hearing the other person. Research published in the International Journal of Auditing confirms that understanding and sharing the speaker's perspective is key to effective communication.

So, how can we become better listeners? Three simple strategies can make a big difference:

- Show genuine interest through non-verbal cues like nodding and maintaining eye contact. These signals reassure the speaker that we're paying attention and care about what they're saying.
- Avoid interpreting or paraphrasing the speaker's words. Instead of saying, "So what you mean is..." which can come across as judgmental, let them express themselves freely without interruption.
- Encourage the speaker to delve deeper into their thoughts and feelings. By asking open-ended questions and showing

empathy, we create a safe space for them to explore their emotions.

By listening attentively and speaking less, we not only understand others better but also empower them to find their own solutions. In the end, the greatest gift we can offer is often the simple act of listening."

Gratitude: The Key to Acknowledging Help

"Shut up about the services you've provided, but talk about the Favors you've received." - Epictetus

How often do we encounter someone who only talks about their own achievements, forgetting the contributions of others? It's a common scenario in both social and professional settings. You might share news about a project or accomplishment, only to hear someone boast about their role in it, leaving you wondering, 'Did they forget the support they received?'

In Stoic philosophy, humility and gratitude are valued virtues. Epictetus reminds us to focus not on boasting about our own actions, but on acknowledging the favors we've received from others. After all, expressing gratitude requires far fewer words than self-praise.

When discussing our successes, it's important to recognize the role of those who have helped us along the way. Saying, 'I owe a lot to my mentors,' or 'My team played a crucial part in this,' carries more meaning and brevity than a lengthy self-congratulatory speech.

Stoicism encourages us to take a step back and view our lives objectively, identifying our mistakes and shortcomings. Similarly, in our conversations, we should consider whether we're driven by ego or gratitude. Choosing gratitude not only reflects Stoic principles but also strengthens relationships and fosters humility."

Pause Before You Speak: Harnessing the Power of Reflection

"Better to falter with your feet than with your tongue." -
Zeno

Ever found yourself in that awkward moment after saying something you wish you hadn't? We've all been there. It's easy to slip up in speech or writing – it's part of being human. But if we let every impulse guide our words, we risk damaging the very relationships we cherish.

Epictetus, a prominent Stoic philosopher, taught us about the concept of control: what we can influence and what we cannot. He emphasized that we have control over our actions and thoughts, including our speech. However, external factors like our reputation or circumstances are beyond our control.

Monitoring our speech requires effort. If it were simple, we'd all be eloquent speakers. Yet, when we realize that our words stem from our own choices, we become accountable for them.

Next time you find yourself in a social setting or heated discussion, try this Stoic practice: count to three before responding. Use this brief pause to consider the impact of your words. Are they clear?

Could they be misinterpreted? Will they add value to the conversation? Often, we react impulsively to what we hear. By pausing, we give ourselves the chance to respond thoughtfully.

Embrace this Stoic discipline, and you'll discover that many of the things we think we need to say are better left unsaid."

Utilize Silence to Defuse Conflict

"You don't have to turn it into something. It mustn't upset you." - Marcus Aurelius

Marcus Aurelius, the Stoic emperor, reminds us that we don't have to let every situation get under our skin. This is especially true in moments of tension when we're tempted to lash out or assert dominance.

Stressful encounters often trigger our impulse to defend ourselves or our beliefs vigorously. But Stoics caution against allowing anger to cloud our judgment, likening it to a form of temporary madness.

When faced with confrontation or criticism, our instinct may be to react defensively. But what are we defending? Often, it's our ego.

A more powerful response, however, lies in silence. Rather than matching the other person's intensity, we can choose to remain calm and composed, much like a matador evading a charging bull. By withholding immediate retaliation and responding at the right moment, we maintain control over the situation.

In the midst of heated exchanges, remember the wisdom of an old German proverb: "The best response to anger is silence." Through silence, we invite reflection and allow both parties to find resolution without escalating the conflict.

Focus on Substance, Not Superficial Talk

Epictetus, a Stoic philosopher, advises us to be mindful of our words. He suggests speaking only when necessary and avoiding trivial topics like entertainment or mundane gossip.

Silence often receives criticism in a world where constant chatter is the norm. Yet, silence can be more valuable than meaningless speech. Imagine if you knew how limited your time truly is – would you spend it discussing trivial matters?

Seneca, another Stoic thinker, emphasizes the importance of quality over quantity in life. This principle applies to our speech as well. Instead of filling conversations with empty words, strive to make each word count. By being selective with what we say, we conserve our energy for meaningful discussions and real problems.

So, the next time you engage in conversation, consider the substance of your words. Focus on making a meaningful contribution rather than simply adding to the noise. In doing so, you'll find greater fulfilment and purpose in your interactions.

Embrace Silence: A Stoic Approach to Overcoming Fear

"Silence is a lesson we have learned from the many sufferings of life" - Seneca

Seneca, a Stoic philosopher, believed that silence teaches us valuable lessons, often learned through life's trials and tribulations. Silence can be a response to fear or a deliberate choice to speak only when words hold true value.

Many people fear speaking out of worry they might say the wrong thing. Surveys over the years consistently rank public speaking and death as top fears. It's a paradox in a society where people would rather avoid speaking than engage in discourse. Stoicism offers a powerful tool to confront such fears: the premeditation of adversity.

The premeditation of adversity is a Stoic exercise where we envision worst-case scenarios, allowing us to confront our fears and build resilience. By imagining our worst fears and experiencing associated emotions, we prepare ourselves to face challenges head-on. This practice aligns with cognitive behavioral therapy, where clients confront their fears to overcome them gradually.

Language errors and the fear of judgment can lead us to silence our voices out of pain rather than strength. But Stoicism teaches us to question the worst that could happen and view fear from a rational perspective. Imagining scenarios like blank slides in a presentation or a rejected manuscript helps put fear into context. In hindsight, such experiences are often less daunting than they seem in the moment.

Marcus Aurelius, another Stoic philosopher, reminds us of our duty to speak truthfully and kindly. Stoic silence isn't about avoiding confrontation but about maintaining composure and wisdom in the face of adversity.

In today's noisy world, cultivating stillness through silence becomes crucial. Amid constant distractions, silence allows us to listen deeply and speak with honesty and clarity. Whether it's offering advice to a friend or facing personal challenges, Stoic silence empowers us to navigate life's complexities with grace and mastery.

CHAPTER 10:
PRACTICAL EXERCISES

Stoic Practices for Navigating Today's Turbulent World

When Zeno found himself stranded in Athens after a shipwreck, it seemed like a stroke of bad luck. However, he turned this adversity into an opportunity for growth. With little else to do, he immersed himself in the teachings of Socrates at a local bookstore. Inspired by the wisdom he found there, Zeno decided to share his newfound knowledge with anyone who would listen.

Thus began the philosophy of stoicism. Zeno's teachings quickly gained popularity, transcending social barriers to reach both the lowly and the powerful. As Zeno later humorously remarked, he "made a prosperous journey when [he] was wrecked."

Yet, the story of stoicism doesn't stop with Zeno. Even today, centuries later, its principles remain as relevant as ever, offering valuable guidance in our fast-paced world. These stoic practices can help us find peace amidst the chaos of modern life.

#1 Cultivate Inner Control

"Man is not disturbed by things, but by the views he takes of them." - Epictetus

A lot of what happens in life is out of our hands. The Stoics understood this truth and focused on what they could control instead.

Take Epictetus, for example. Born into slavery and facing physical limitations due to a broken leg inflicted by his master, he had every reason to feel powerless. He lived a life of poverty with little control over his external circumstances.

Yet, Epictetus didn't see it that way. He believed that his thoughts, desires, and dislikes were still his own, even if he couldn't control his possessions or his body. These were aspects of life he considered within his domain.

In today's world, it's easy to get frustrated over minor inconveniences. We're so accustomed to comfort that even small disruptions can trigger irritation or anger. Whether it's a slow internet connection or a brief traffic delay, our natural response tends to be negative.

But it's not the external events themselves that make us unhappy; it's our chosen emotional reactions to them. The key is recognizing that we have the power to control our psychological state regardless of what's happening around us.

Once we internalize this mindset, we realize that our happiness isn't dependent on external circumstances. We have the ability to find contentment and peace within ourselves, no matter what life throws our way.

#2 Guard Your Time

"We are rich in property and money, yet we often squander time without much thought. It's the one thing we should be most frugal with." - Seneca

The Stoics recognized that time is our most valuable asset. Unlike our material possessions, once time is lost, it can never be regained. Therefore, we should strive to waste as little of it as possible.

Those who fritter away this precious resource on trivial matters or entertainment will eventually realize that they have nothing substantial to show for it. Procrastination and putting things off will eventually catch up with us because tomorrow is never guaranteed.

Conversely, those who freely give away their time to others without careful consideration may find themselves no better off than those who waste it. Many of us allow our time to be hijacked by people and obligations without truly reflecting on the implications. This is where using calendars and schedules wisely becomes crucial. They should serve us, not enslave us.

No matter the nature of our commitments, time remains invaluable. We might think we have plenty of it, but in reality, it's a finite resource that should be cherished and managed wisely.

#3 Prioritize Your Own Well-being

"I have often wondered how it is that every man loves himself more than all the rest of men, but yet sets less value on his own opinions of himself than on the opinions of others." - Marcus Aurelius

A significant part of our actions stems from our innate desire for acceptance and approval from others. In ancient times, being accepted by our social group was crucial for survival. Rejection could mean isolation or even death.

To some extent, this still holds true today. But how much of our time and energy do we invest in seeking validation from others?

We often spend money we don't have on unnecessary luxuries just to impress people we don't genuinely care about. Our career choices and lifestyles are often influenced by how others perceive us rather than what truly fulfills us. We unknowingly become hostages to society's expectations, paying a hefty price without any guarantee of freedom.

In contrast, the Roman statesman Cato pursued a life independent of others' opinions. He dressed oddly and walked barefoot in the streets as a way of teaching himself to be ashamed only of things worthy of shame, disregarding other forms of humiliation.

This mindset empowered him to stand firm against Julius Caesar's excessive power, enabling him to make important decisions without fear of disapproval.

There's much to learn from Cato's example. It's far better to live life on our own terms and disregard the judgments of others. Happiness should never be dependent on external validation.

#4 Maintain Your Focus Amid Distractions

"If one does not know to which port one is sailing, no wind is favorable." - Seneca

Modern society offers us a plethora of opportunities. From dining out to traveling to entertainment, we have more options available to us than ever before. However, this abundance hasn't necessarily led to better outcomes. In fact, the sheer number of choices can often leave us feeling paralyzed by indecision.

Our brains haven't evolved at the same pace as technological advancements, and we find ourselves inundated with an overwhelming amount of information. The difficulty of making decisions in such a cluttered environment often leads us to default to the status quo.

This dilemma is a fundamental challenge we encounter in our daily lives. With so many options, we struggle to commit to a particular course of action. We either procrastinate making decisions or try to juggle multiple activities simultaneously, resulting in little to no progress.

The Stoics emphasized the importance of focused action. It's not enough to simply react to our circumstances; we must live with intentionality and purposefully direct our efforts toward our goals.

#5 Let Go of Ego and Vanity

"Get rid of your presumptions, for it's impossible for someone to begin learning what they think they already know." - Epictetus

Epictetus, as a teacher, often felt frustrated by students who claimed to seek education but secretly believed they already knew everything. This is a common challenge for educators and a trait many of us can relate to: the tendency towards ego and arrogance, thinking we've learned enough and are superior to others.

This mindset is particularly risky in today's world. The information we have at our fingertips may not only be insufficient for solving tomorrow's problems but could also hinder our ability to think critically. In a constantly evolving environment, as Marcus Aurelius noted,

"The universe is in flux; life is a matter of opinion."

That's why many of today's brightest minds devote much of their time to reading and learning. They recognize that wisdom can be found in the past, present, and future.

It would be wise for us to follow suit, adopting a mindset of perpetual learning. We should always strive to remain humble students, open to new ideas and perspectives.

#6 Organize Your Thoughts Through Writing

"No one has ever become wise by accident." - Seneca

Among the many tasks we perform each day, none is as crucial as taking a moment to introspect. Engaging in self-reflection compels us to confront ourselves and examine our beliefs about the world. It's through this process that answers to some of life's most significant questions emerge.

Keeping a journal remains one of the most effective methods of self-awareness. It fosters creativity, enhances gratitude, and serves as a form of therapy. The benefits are numerous. When you put your thoughts and feelings into writing, they become clearer than they ever could be just in your mind.

The Stoics understood the power of journaling. Marcus Aurelius, one of the most powerful men in the Roman Empire, consistently took the time to record his observations and emotions, whether in times of war or peace.

While today, everyone from athletes to entrepreneurs benefits from Marcus Aurelius's wisdom, it's evident that the greatest beneficiary of his writing and introspection was himself. The clarity of thought and accountability that his journaling brought about helped him maintain his virtue, even in a position where others might have succumbed to error and tyranny.

So, take the time to journal. It's not a difficult task, and the rewards it brings are immense.

#7 Stand Firm in Your Beliefs

"By doing nothing, you learn to do evil." - Cato

In a world where compromise was often seen as necessary, Cato stood out for his unwavering commitment to his principles. He believed that all virtues were interconnected and that all vices were equally damaging.

Some might argue that Cato set an impossibly high standard. Indeed, many accomplishments require compromises. However, in today's world, it seems that we often sacrifice our principles in the name of tolerance or financial gain.

Cato's refusal to compromise angered both his allies and his adversaries. He expected those close to him to adopt the same steadfast attitude, leaving no room for flexibility. Yet, his adherence to this unyielding standard earned him unwavering respect and authority. He became Rome's moral compass, distinguishing between right and wrong.

While not all of us can emulate Cato's exact approach, there's a valuable lesson to be learned. If we never stand firm in our beliefs, we risk losing ourselves to everything and anything.

#8 Envision the Worst-Case Scenario

"Nothing happens to the wise man against his expectation."
- Seneca

In recent times, there's been much talk about the power of positive thinking. We're often told that optimism and affirmations lead to a happier life. But the Stoics took a different approach.

They believed that such practices could lead to passivity, encouraging us to simply wait for things to improve rather than taking proactive steps. Instead of sugarcoating reality, they advocated for active participation.

One of their common practices, known as "premeditatio malorum," involves mentally preparing for the worst-case scenarios. This entails visualizing the most adverse outcomes that could occur — whether it's a significant loss, financial ruin, or even death.

By asking questions like, "What if everything went wrong tomorrow? How would I handle it? Should this affect how I live today?" the Stoics sought to mentally prepare themselves for potential hardships.

This exercise yielded valuable insights and benefits. It helped them take precautions to prevent undesired outcomes from materializing. Even if they did encounter failure, they were better equipped to navigate it because they had already considered how to survive adversity.

Ultimately, this approach allowed them to prepare for success while also being resilient in the face of failure.

#9 Recognize the Impermanence of All Things

"Alexander the Great and his mule both died, and the same thing happened to both." - Marcus Aurelius

In the grand scheme of things, nothing we achieve holds lasting significance.

It's a notion that prompts reflection. We tend to perceive ourselves as central figures in the universe, creating an illusion of our own importance. We see ourselves as protagonists in our own stories.

However, this perception is merely a construct of our minds. While those around us may share similar sentiments, in the long run, each of us is ultimately insignificant. Even the brightest minds, such as Edison and Newton, would eventually fade into footnotes in history.

We shouldn't succumb to irrational expectations or external pressures, nor should we chase goals solely to leave behind a legacy. None of us will ultimately carry such things with us.

What truly matters is living life on our own terms. This is the path to experiencing true fulfillment.

10 Natural Training Exercises for a Traditional Lifestyle

The Stoics placed great emphasis on practical application in their philosophy.

Contrary to what you might think, Stoic exercises aren't just academic or theoretical; they're deeply relevant in today's world. These practices offer practical guidance and wisdom that have endured for over two millennia, shaping individuals and societies.

Engaging in daily Stoic exercises can transform you into a better person and friend. They teach you to react with less emotion and prepare you to face life's challenges, whether they're minor annoyances or major setbacks, with inner peace.

These exercises equip us to strive for a good life, maintain composure and perseverance in tough times, and navigate our fast-paced world more effectively.

It's time to embrace these benefits and cultivate a calmer, more resilient approach to daily life.

Before delving into the ten Stoic exercises, it's important to understand the significance of practicing Stoicism.

Practical Stoicism: Philosophy in Action

Stoic practices aren't just about acquiring knowledge; they're about applying and embodying that wisdom in everyday life.

Epictetus wisely cautioned against merely learning without putting knowledge into practice. He emphasized the importance of continuous training, as we tend to forget what we've learned over time and may inadvertently act in ways contrary to our beliefs.

Just as in sports, mastery comes through consistent practice. By engaging in Stoic exercises regularly, you can significantly improve your quality of life.

The Stoics viewed themselves as spiritual warriors, dedicated to applying Stoicism in their daily lives. They believed philosophy should be lived, not merely studied, and they practiced it diligently, day in and day out.

It's not enough to simply understand Stoic principles; you must actively incorporate them into your life. These exercises aren't passive observations—they require active participation and practice.

Remember, we're all unique, and different Stoic exercises may resonate more with different individuals. The key is to find what works best for you and commit to regular practice.

Therefore, the following exercises should be considered as suggestions. Try those who speak to you.

#1 Stoic Exercise: Who's Your Role Model?

"Choose someone whose lifestyle and his words have obtained your approval. Always indicate it to yourself, as your tutor or as a model. From my point of view, someone is needed as a yardstick with which our characters can measure themselves. Without a sovereign who does it against you, it will not go wrong. "- Seneca

The Stoics encouraged the use of role models, particularly the stoic sage—an epitome of virtue and excellence who lives a tranquil and fulfilling life. While this sage is an ideal yet hypothetical figure, we often find it more practical to choose a well-known role model closer to our reality.

Enter Batman. Or anyone else you admire and respect. The key is to select someone whose lifestyle and values resonate with you.

Here's how the Stoic practice works: When faced with a tough decision or challenging situation, ask yourself, "What would Batman do?" Or, depending on the circumstance, you might consider, "What would the perfect father do?" "What would your ideal friend do?" or "What would the best boss do?"

By considering the actions of your chosen role model, you can gain insight into how to navigate difficult situations with wisdom and virtue.

#2 Stoic Exercise: Negative Visualization

"What is not expected has a worse impact, and the unexpected increases the weight of a disaster. The fact that it was unexpected has always increased a person's pain. We should project our thoughts in front of us in every curve and keep an eye on all possible eventualities instead of the usual sequence of events. "- Seneca

Negative visualization is a well-known Stoic practice aimed at preparing ourselves for potential challenges in the future.

In essence, it involves imagining possible negative outcomes or future scenarios to mentally prepare for them. By doing so, we equip ourselves to remain calm and respond effectively when faced with adversity.

As Seneca wisely noted, unexpected events can be doubly painful. Therefore, it's beneficial to anticipate and be ready for potential hardships. While experiencing a setback may still be unpleasant, knowing it could happen helps us handle it with greater composure.

Here's how the Stoic exercise works: Find a comfortable space and reflect on potential unfortunate scenarios:

Are you planning an event like exams, vacations, business presentations, or weddings? Consider what could go wrong.

Think about your choices. What if your plans suddenly fall through? How would you react?

Additionally, contemplate your mortality. What if you were to pass away unexpectedly? How would you feel? Imagining this worst-case scenario can help put things into perspective and remind us of the importance of making the most of our time.

#3 Stoic Exercise: Voluntary Discomfort - Starbucks Floor Challenge

"Take a certain number of days to settle for the cheapest and cheapest fare, with a rough and rough dress, and say to yourself," Is this the condition I was afraid of? "It is precisely in times of immunity to worry that the soul will strengthen on occasions of greater stress, and it is just as fortunate that it strengthens against its violence ... If you do

not win a man if the crisis arrives, train him before he arrives." - Seneca

Voluntary discomfort is a Stoic practice aimed at preparing ourselves for unpleasant situations so we can face them with resilience when they arise.

The idea is to deliberately push ourselves outside of our comfort zones to expand our capacity to handle discomfort. For instance, if you typically feel uneasy when you can't eat for an extended period, you might practice intermittent fasting for 48 hours once a month. Over time, this can help desensitize you to the discomfort of going without food for shorter periods.

Here's how the Stoic exercise works: Intentionally expose yourself to discomfort on a regular basis. One suggestion, inspired by Tim Ferriss, is the Starbucks Floor Challenge:

Spend a night sleeping on the floor to experience discomfort and appreciate the simplicity of life.

Challenge yourself to ask for a 10% discount when ordering coffee, or go without coffee for a week to break a comfort habit.

By intentionally subjecting ourselves to discomfort in controlled settings, we can better prepare ourselves to handle unexpected challenges with grace and resilience.

#4 Stoic Exercise: Add a Reservation Clause

"I will cross the sea if nothing prevents me." - Seneca

Stoics understand that not everything is within our control. So, they incorporate reservation clauses into their actions—a reminder of humility and acceptance of uncertainty.

This practice acknowledges that while we may plan and strive for certain outcomes, external factors beyond our control can influence the results. It's a way of mentally preparing ourselves for the unpredictability of life.

A similar concept is found in Muslim culture, where the phrase "Inshallah" (if Allah wills) is commonly used. This phrase encompasses two key aspects: giving your best effort while recognizing that the ultimate outcome is determined by a higher power.

Here's how the exercise works: When making plans or decisions, add a reservation clause such as "if nothing prevents me," "Deo volente," "Inshallah," or "God willing." This serves as a reminder to approach life with humility and acceptance of the unknown.

#5 Stoic Exercise: Embrace Your Fate - Love Your Destiny

"Destiny guides the will and drags on with the reluctant." - Seneca

The Stoics focused on what they could control, and fate wasn't one of those things. Instead of wishing for reality to be different, they advised accepting and embracing it.

They often used the metaphor of a dog on a leash attached to a moving cart. A wise person, like a content dog, walks alongside the cart happily, while a foolish one, like a resisting dog, is dragged along unhappily.

In life, we can't change what happens to us. So it's wiser to accept our circumstances rather than fighting against them. We're like the dog on the leash: our freedom is limited, and struggling against reality only leads to unhappiness.

The Stoic exercise goes like this: When faced with a situation, ask yourself if there's anything you can do to change it. If not, accept it as part of your fate. Resisting reality only causes suffering.

Practice non-resistance: Don't wish for reality to be different. Avoid judgment: Accept events as they are without passing judgment on them. Practice detachment: Recognize that things come and go, so don't become too attached to what you desire.

#6 Stoic Exercise: Pain and Illness - A Chance for Virtue

"Illness is an obstacle for the body, but not for the will unless the will itself decides. Limp is an obstacle for the leg, but not for the will. And discuss this myth on the occasion of everything that happened; because you will find an obstacle for something else, but not for yourself." - Epictetus

Epictetus, a Stoic teacher, was physically challenged, but he saw his condition as a hindrance for his leg, not for his mind.

Similarly, pain and illness affect the body, not the mind. We have the power to choose how we respond to pain. We can bravely endure it or succumb to complaints and self-pity. The choice is ours to make.

This exercise encourages us not to give in to weakness or self-pity when experiencing pain. Such reactions only worsen the situation.

Here's how it works: The next time you feel pain, use it as an opportunity to strengthen your virtue. Remember, pain is felt by the body, not the mind.

Got a headache? View it as a chance to cultivate resilience.

Feeling under the weather? Allow your body to rest without complaining. Refuse to let pain overpower you and strive to maintain inner calm.

#7 Stoic Exercise: Viewing Possessions as Borrowed

"We have no reason to admire ourselves as if our possessions surrounded us; We have been lent. We like to use and enjoy them, but who made the gift decides how long we should be tenants; It is our duty to keep the gifts that we have received indefinitely and return them without complaint when requested. He is a sad debtor who abuses his creditor." - Seneca

According to Seneca, everything we own is essentially on loan to us. Our possessions, our loved ones, our very lives—they can all be taken away in an instant.

As Stoics, we should cherish these things while we have them, but we must also recognize their impermanence. We should see them as borrowed—whether from nature, luck, or a higher power—and understand that we can only enjoy them temporarily. They can be taken away at any moment, without warning.

Seneca questioned why we often fail to consider the possibility of loss, despite witnessing misfortunes around us. It's a form of ignorance.

Here's how the Stoic practice works: Remind yourself that everything you possess, even if you've paid for it, is not truly yours. Be aware that anything dear to you can be taken away without notice.

Reflect on your favorite possessions or relationships, and imagine them disappearing tomorrow. When bidding farewell to loved ones, contemplate the possibility that it could be the last time you see them.

#8 Stoic Exercise: Appreciate Your Blessings

"Don't focus on things you don't own as if they were yours, but count the blessings you have and think how much you would like them if they weren't already yours. But be careful that you don't appreciate these things so much that you worry if you lose them." - Marcus Aurelius

The Stoics embraced minimalism, valuing what they had instead of longing for what they lacked. They practiced gratitude for the blessings in their lives, finding contentment in what they already possessed rather than desiring more.

Here's how the exercise works:

- Acknowledge the tendency to accumulate possessions unnecessarily.
- Express gratitude for what you already have without becoming overly attached to these things, recognizing that they could be taken away at any moment.
- Reflect on the things you currently have and imagine how much you would desire them if they were not already in your possession.

Similar to other Stoic practices, you can write down the things you're thankful for. For instance, jot down three things you appreciate.

The key is to avoid unnecessary consumption, appreciate what you already have, and maintain a healthy detachment from material possessions.

#9 Stoic Exercise: Practice Forgiveness - Recognize Ignorance in Others

"If a person accepts the wrong, then he knows that he did not want to accept the wrong: 'Because no soul is deprived of the truth with its consent,' as Plato says, but the wrong seemed true to him." - Epictetus

The Stoics believed that everyone acts according to what they believe is right, even if they are mistaken. While their actions may cause harm, they do not intend to do wrong.

Instead of blaming others for their actions, the Stoics encouraged empathy and understanding. We should feel compassion for them rather than resentment.

How can we hold grudges against someone who acted out of ignorance? Instead, we should strive to be tolerant and compassionate, as Jesus taught: "Father, forgive them, for they know not what they do."

Here's how the Stoic exercise works: Before reacting angrily to someone's actions, remind yourself that they may not have known any better. Choose kindness and forgiveness instead of seeking revenge.

Rather than blaming others, view their actions as an opportunity for personal growth. Just like in physical training, mistakes happen, but we learn from them and continue to improve. So, brush off the negativity and move forward with grace.

#10 Stoic Exercise: Invest in Inner Peace

"Start with things of little value - some spilled oil, some stolen wine - and repeat for yourself: 'For such a low price, I can buy peace of mind.'" - Epictetus

This concept is truly insightful.

One of the primary goals of Stoicism is to maintain inner calm amidst challenging situations. Regardless of what happens, Stoics aim to remain composed and rational.

"I'm purchasing tranquility instead." This mantra has spared me from wasting energy and emotions on countless occasions. When faced with circumstances that provoke frustration or agitation, I often remind myself: "I'm investing in peace instead."

This principle extends to all facets of life, as I've learned from various Stoic readings. I highly recommend incorporating this mindset into your daily routine—it's transformative.

The only requirement is developing enough self-awareness to shift from reaction to response. With practice, you'll swiftly reap the benefits of these words.

Here's how the Stoic exercise works: Bring mindfulness to your experiences and remind yourself that when faced with irritation or dissatisfaction, you're choosing to invest in inner peace instead.

If you spill wine on your clothes, invest in peace instead.

If your roommate neglects to wash the dishes, invest in peace instead.

If your favorite sports team disappoints, invest in peace instead.

The Stoics Practiced the So-Called "Spiritual Exercises" And Gained Strength from Them.

Let's take a look at nine of the essential exercises.

#1 Practical Training for Adversity

> *"In times of safety, the mind should prepare for difficult times; while happiness favors it, it is time to be strengthened against their waste." - Seneca*

Seneca, a wealthy advisor to Nero, proposed a practical approach to facing adversity. He recommended setting aside a few days each month to simulate poverty. During these days, one would limit themselves to basic necessities, wear shabby clothes, refrain from comforts of home, and even sleep on the floor. By immersing oneself in such conditions, Seneca believed one could confront their fears and ask, "Was I truly afraid of this?"

It's crucial to understand that this exercise isn't just a mental game—it's about living through hardship. Seneca argued that excessive comfort can enslave us, as we constantly fear losing it. However, by actively preparing for adversity, we diminish its power to disrupt our lives.

Montaigne, a philosopher, appreciated an ancient drinking game where participants alternated between viewing a painting of a corpse in a coffin and raising a glass in celebration. The message was clear: "Drink and be happy, for one day you'll look like this."

Emotions like fear often stem from insecurity and unfamiliarity. Those who have faced their fears firsthand know the drain these emotions can have on energy. The solution lies in confronting ignorance. By familiarizing ourselves with what we fear, either through mental simulations or real-life experiences, we realize that most disadvantages are temporary and reversible.

#2 Train Your Perception to Avoid Feeling Hurt By Ethical or Evil Actions

"Choose not to harm yourself, and you won't feel harmed. If you don't feel harmed, then you haven't been." - Marcus Aurelius

The Stoics had a practice called "Overthrow the obstacle." Their aim was to make it impossible not to engage in philosophical thinking. The idea was that by flipping a problem on its head, every challenge could be seen as an opportunity for growth.

Imagine you're trying to help someone, but they respond with grumpiness or reluctance. Instead of letting it frustrate you, Stoic philosophy suggests seeing it as a chance to cultivate virtues like patience or understanding.

"The obstacle to action guides the action. What blocks the path becomes the path." - Marcus Aurelius

This concept is reminiscent of what Obama referred to as "teachable moments." When faced with Reverend Wright's scandal, Obama turned it into an opportunity to address issues of race in America.

Entrepreneurs often miss out on opportunities because they fail to recognize them. For Stoics, everything can be seen as an opportunity for growth, whether it's a challenging situation where your efforts are unappreciated or the loss of a loved one. Stoics believe there's neither good nor bad inherently; it's all about perception, which you can control. If you can detach your initial response from disappointment, you'll find that every situation presents an opportunity for growth.

This exercise inspired the book "The Obstacle Is The Way."

#3 Everything is Temporary

"Alexander the Great and his charioteer both died, and the same fate awaited both." -Marcus Aurelius

Marcus Aurelius had a useful practice to regain perspective and maintain balance:

"Think about all those who were once famous, unfortunate, despised, or just ordinary. Where are they now? They've become nothing more than smoke, dust, or forgotten legends. Consider all these examples. How insignificant are the things we desire so passionately?"

It's important to note that when Stoics talk about "passion," they're not referring to modern enthusiasm but rather to strong emotions like anger. What's crucial is to replace these with healthier emotions, like finding joy instead of excessive excitement.

Returning to the earlier point: remember how small you are, and how small almost everything else is. Successes can be fleeting, here one moment and gone the next. But if everything is temporary, does it really matter?

What matters is being a good person and making the right choices in the present moment, which was significant for the Stoics.

Take the example of Alexander the Great, who conquered vast territories and had cities named after him. Yet, even he faced personal struggles. The Stoics pointed out that Alexander accidentally killed his closest friend, Cleitus, in a drunken fight. This led to intense grief and self-imposed suffering for Alexander.

Is this the mark of a successful life? From a Stoic perspective, having your name celebrated means little if you lose sight of what truly matters and cause harm to those around you.

Learn from Alexander's mistake. Cultivate humility, honesty, and self-awareness. These qualities are within your control and can be nurtured every day of your life. You need not fear losing them or having them taken from you by others.

#4 Gain a Broader Perspective

"As Plato eloquently stated, when discussing human affairs, it's best to have a bird's-eye view and see everything at once - from gatherings, battles, farms, weddings and divorces, births and deaths, bustling classrooms or quiet rooms, all strangers, holidays, monuments, markets: all intertwined and arranged in opposition." - Marcus Aurelius

Marcus often practiced an exercise known as "Top View" or "Plato's View." He encourages us to step back, zoom out, and see life from a higher vantage point than our own. This exercise, envisioning countless people engaged in various activities like "armies, farms, marriages and divorces, births and deaths," helps us gain perspective and, like the previous exercise, reminds us of our smallness. It reorients us, as the Stoic Pierre Hadot noted: "Seeing from above changes our evaluations of things: luxury, power, war... and the everyday worries seem trivial."

The second, more subtle, point is to tap into what the Stoics refer to as sympathy or interconnectedness with all humanity. Like astronaut Edgar Mitchell, one of the first people to experience a "view from above," who said: "In space, there's an instant global consciousness, a human orientation, an intense dissatisfaction with the state of the world, and a compulsion to do something about it." Take a step back from your concerns and remember your responsibility to others. Embrace Plato's perspective.

#5 Remember You Will Die: Reflect on Your Mortality

"We shape our thoughts as if we've reached the end of our lives. We don't leave anything unresolved. Every day, we strive to balance the ledger of life." - Seneca

Seneca's quote encapsulates Memento Mori - an ancient practice of contemplating mortality dating back to Socrates, who believed that true philosophy was essentially practicing how to die. In his reflections, Marcus Aurelius wrote: "You could leave life right now. Let that determine what you do, say, and think." It served as a personal reminder to live virtuously without delay.

Stoics find this idea both empowering and humbling. It's no wonder that one of Seneca's biographies is titled "Dying Every Day," as he encouraged us to say "You may not wake up tomorrow" before going to bed and "You may not fall asleep again" upon waking, to remind us of our mortality. Similarly, Epictetus, another Stoic, urged his students to "Keep death and exile before your eyes every day, along with anything else that seems dreadful - if you do, you'll never have a base thought or desire."

These daily reminders and meditations serve as the foundation for living life to the fullest and not wasting a single moment. Let them guide you in making the most of every day.

#6 "Can I Control It?"

"The main goal in life is simply to recognize and distinguish things so that we can clearly determine which external factors are beyond my control and which relate to the decisions I can actually influence. Where should I direct my attention? To what is good and bad? Not to the uncontrollable external events, but inwardly to the decisions that are within my power..." - Epictetus

The central practice in Stoic philosophy is to discern between what we can change and what we cannot. What we can affect and what is beyond our influence. For instance, if a flight is delayed due to bad weather, no amount of yelling at the airline representative will stop the storm. Similarly, no amount of wishing will alter our height, nationality, or other unchangeable aspects of life. Moreover, the time spent fretting over these unchangeable circumstances detracts from addressing the things we can actually influence.

Return to this question daily, especially in challenging situations. Make it a habit to reflect on it regularly. By focusing on clarifying which aspects of your day are within your control and which are not, you not only cultivate greater contentment but also gain a distinct advantage over others who may not realize they are grappling with an unwinnable battle.

#7 Journaling

Epictetus, the former slave. Marcus Aurelius, the emperor. Seneca, the statesman and playwright. These three men led vastly different lives, yet they shared a common practice: journaling.

Each had their own approach. Epictetus advised his students to make philosophy a daily habit, emphasizing the importance of writing every day as a form of mental training. Seneca preferred to reflect on his day in the evening, after his household had settled down. He would review everything he had done and said, leaving nothing hidden or ignored. He found that sleeping after this personal examination was particularly gratifying. And Marcus Aurelius, perhaps the most prolific of them all, diligently recorded his thoughts and reflections, which have been preserved for us under the title "Meditations."

Journaling is a way to reflect on the day that has passed, to recall the wisdom imparted by our teachers, our readings, and our own experiences. Merely hearing these lessons once is not enough; we must practice them repeatedly, turning them over in our minds, and, most importantly, writing them down to feel their flow through our fingers.

In this way, journaling becomes intertwined with Stoicism. It's nearly impossible to separate the two.

#8 Practice Negative Visualization

Negative visualization, also known as "premeditatio malorum" or "pre-meditation of evil," is a Stoic exercise where we imagine potential misfortunes or losses. This practice helps us prepare for life's inevitable setbacks. We don't always get what we want, even if we deserve it. Life is not always straightforward and predictable. Psychologically preparing for this reality is crucial. It's one of the most potent tools in the Stoic toolkit for cultivating resilience and inner strength.

For instance, Seneca would begin by reviewing or envisioning his plans, such as embarking on a journey. Then, he would mentally analyze potential obstacles or disasters: a storm could arise, the captain might fall ill, or the ship could be attacked by pirates.

"Nothing happens to the wise person contrary to their expectation," he wrote to a friend, "...everything turns out as they wished, not as they calculated - but most importantly, they calculated that something could disrupt their plans."

Through this exercise, Seneca was always prepared for adversity and integrated it into his plans. He was ready for both victory and defeat.

#9 Amor Fati: Embrace Everything that Happens

The renowned German philosopher Friedrich Nietzsche coined the term "amor fati" to describe his outlook on life - a love of fate. He advocated accepting everything as it is, without wishing for anything to be different. The Stoics not only understood this mindset but also embraced it. Two thousand years ago, the Emperor Marcus Aurelius wrote in his personal diary, later known as "Meditations," that,

"A blazing fire turns all it touches into flame and light."
Despite facing numerous adversities, he repeated the
mantra: "Don't seek things to happen as you wish; wish for
them to happen as they do: then you will be happy."

Amor Fati, therefore, is the Stoic practice and mentality of making the most of every situation. It involves treating each moment, no matter how challenging, as something to be accepted rather than avoided. Not only accepting it but loving it and becoming better because of it. Just as oxygen fuels a fire, obstacles and adversities become opportunities for growth and potential.

Stoicism is practical for real-life situations. Stoic writings candidly discuss how to become better individuals, find happiness, and confront the problems we encounter. They show how facing adversity strengthens us, how turning obstacles into opportunities empowers us, and how remembering our own insignificance keeps our egos in check and provides perspective.

Ultimately, Stoicism isn't a grand philosophical discourse on the nature of existence. It's a collection of reflections, advice, and tools for living a good life. As Marcus Aurelius noted, Stoicism isn't a masterful teacher but rather a soothing balm, a helpful remedy for the wounds we encounter in life. Epictetus aptly described life as challenging and unforgiving, but Stoicism offers guidance on how to navigate its difficulties.

CHAPTER 11: STOICISM DRUGS

Stoicism for Coping with Trauma, Chronic Illness, and Overall Health and Happiness

Stoicism is an ancient philosophy that originated with Zeno of Citium in ancient Greece and later gained prominence in the Roman Empire. For individuals dealing with trauma, navigating daily life can be challenging. Traumatic events can leave lasting mental, emotional, and psychological scars.

Similarly, those with chronic illnesses face numerous hurdles, including stigma, criticism, and even bullying, on top of managing their health issues. Coping with chronic conditions can take a toll mentally and emotionally, often leading to setbacks and frustrations as one searches for solutions.

Stoicism offers a practical approach for tackling these difficult circumstances. By embracing stoic principles and accepting the reality of their conditions, individuals can adopt a more objective outlook and seek ways to improve both their health and their overall well-being.

Personal experiences have shown that it's easy to succumb to bitterness, anger, and cynicism when facing chronic illnesses due to mistreatment or societal attitudes. Stoic practices such as meditation, reflection, and philosophical contemplation can complement other spiritual or physical exercises, providing solace and guidance through emotional, mental, and spiritual challenges.

Despite the adversity posed by chronic illnesses, they need not define or overshadow one's life. In fact, confronting such trials often brings out the best in individuals, fostering personal growth and resilience.

Establishing a routine of morning and evening meditation can be particularly beneficial. Morning meditation involves visualizing the day ahead, acknowledging potential obstacles, and setting intentions. Throughout the day, integrating stoic principles into thoughts and actions can aid in personal development. Finally, evening meditation offers an opportunity to reflect on the day's events, assess successes and failures, and make adjustments for continuous improvement.

By incorporating stoic practices into daily life, individuals can cultivate resilience, gain insight from setbacks, and strive towards a more fulfilling existence.

Treating Social Anxiety: Cognitive Behavioral Therapy and Stoicism

Social anxiety disorder, or social phobia, is the fear or discomfort of being around other people. It's a broad condition with various specific fears associated with it. In this section, we'll explore some effective treatment options.

One of the primary treatments is psychotherapy, with cognitive-behavioral therapy (CBT) being the key method. CBT is particularly effective and quicker in yielding results compared to other therapies. There are two main reasons for this.

Firstly, CBT involves setting clear goals from the beginning, typically deciding on the duration of treatment upfront. This clarity helps focus the therapy, with the average number of sessions being around 16. In contrast, other therapies like psychoanalysis can stretch on for years.

Secondly, CBT is structured and educational, often involving homework assignments between sessions. This active participation from the patient is crucial for success. Unlike some other therapies, CBT has a finite duration, making the treatment more focused and time-efficient.

Some therapists also incorporate stoic principles into their treatment approach. This involves accepting problems calmly and working towards solutions rather than getting caught up in worry or anger. The idea is to avoid making the problem worse by dwelling on it excessively.

It's important for therapists to reassure patients that overcoming social anxiety disorder or any fear-based condition isn't solely reliant on willpower. Patients shouldn't feel dismissed with phrases like "just stop worrying" or "everyone has problems." Instead, they should be empowered to work through their challenges with effective strategies.

The effects of long-term medications are still largely unclear, especially considering that different drugs work differently for different individuals. There's no one-size-fits-all solution. However, in cases of acute distress, such as when someone is close to suicide, medication may be necessary to help calm them down.

There are three main types of medications used for anxiety: anxiolytics, beta-blockers, and antidepressants. Anxiolytics include drugs like Xanax (alprazolam), Klonopin (clonazepam), and Valium (diazepam). Antidepressants such as Zoloft (sertraline),

Wellbutrin (bupropion), and Cymbalta (duloxetine) are also commonly used. Beta-blockers, primarily designed for heart conditions, can also be effective for anxiety. Propranolol, discovered in the late 1950s, is one example, along with esmolol, atenolol, and acebutolol.

It's important to note that what works for one person may not work for another. Working closely with your doctor is essential to find the right medication for you. Sometimes, people may take a medication for months without seeing any positive effects, or even experiencing negative effects, simply because the doctor thinks it might help. However, it's crucial for patients to be proactive in their treatment and communicate with their doctor if the prescribed medication isn't working for them, so they can find an alternative that suits their needs.

Why Being Stoic Helps You?

Being stoic means staying indifferent to both pain and pleasure. When you're excessively joyful, it's easy to lose your balance because joy and sadness often alternate. Similarly, if you're overwhelmed by sadness, only you can help yourself overcome it. Therefore, it's crucial to work on yourself in this aspect. Being stoic can greatly benefit you in various ways. Let's explore some key points.

Stoicism helps you maintain calm and composure in happy or sad situations. Why? Because when you're stoic, you accept that life doesn't always provide smooth sailing or perfect conditions. If you embrace this mindset, you'll find it easier to navigate through life's ups and downs.

Being stoic is particularly valuable during tough times. Whether you face financial losses, the death of a loved one, divorce, job loss, conflicts with friends or enemies, or persistent challenges, stoicism can help you manage these situations more effectively. While these circumstances may be difficult to handle, a stoic approach enables you to emerge from them with resilience and clarity.

Consider how being stoic could have impacted moments of joy, such as birthday celebrations, weddings, or the birth of a child. While it's okay to express happiness, practicing stoicism prevents you from becoming overly attached to fleeting emotions, allowing your mind and heart to remain steady.

In both happy and sad times, maintaining a stoic attitude demonstrates strength and courage. Even when your heart feels heavy, projecting an outward appearance of composure prevents others from sensing your inner turmoil. In doing so, you exhibit resilience and maintain dignity amidst adversity.

In summary, embracing stoicism during both joyful and sorrowful moments can lead to a more balanced and fulfilling life. While others may initially find your lack of overt emotional display surprising, they'll come to appreciate your steadfastness and authenticity. Remember, the journey of life is yours to navigate, and choosing to be stoic empowers you to face its challenges with grace and resilience.

Unlocking the Strength of Stoic Manhood

"Some things are within our control, and some are not. The things we control are our opinions, aspirations, desires, dislikes, and, in essence, our actions. The things we can't control include our bodies, possessions, reputation, and authority – essentially, anything beyond our actions." -
Epictetus

In the teachings of our mentor, Epictetus, lies the path to true manhood that we must strive to embody.

You entered this world for a purpose, greeted by the joy of your family and loved ones. Your upbringing shapes you, with your mother nurturing and your father guiding. While your mother provides love and sustenance, it's your father's role to instill courage and discipline, molding you into a master of authentic male strength.

Yet, there are circumstances where a father may be absent, leaving a void that can lead to rebellion and arrogance in adulthood. This chapter speaks to those who have lost their fathers or yearn for paternal understanding in navigating the complexities of life and becoming resilient men.

Who embodies Stoicism, and how can you become a true man?

A "stoic" is someone who displays minimal emotion and speaks sparingly. Stoicism, a philosophy originating from Zeno of Citium in Greece, was embodied as a way of life by figures like Epictetus, who was born into slavery in Hierapolis, Phrygia (now Turkey). Despite facing immense hardships, Epictetus never complained and applied stoic principles to his life. Even when his master broke his leg, he calmly remarked, "I told you I would break it."

Through Epictetus's example, we can learn to cultivate the qualities of a genuine stoic man.

To embark on the journey of becoming a stoic man, let's delve into understanding who this person truly is. It means embracing a serene and calm demeanor amidst the changes and challenges life throws your way. It involves mastering control over your thoughts and actions, rather than being swayed by external influences.

Here are some key teachings from Epictetus that serve as daily reminders:

- Reflect on the inevitability of death and adversity, keeping them in mind daily to ward off negative thoughts and excessive desires.
- Recognize that life is a constant struggle, and the only escape is through death. Stoics view external desires such as wealth, status, or relationships as indifferent.
- Practice envisioning how a wise and serene deity like Zeus would handle sudden situations, as taught by Epictetus during his lectures in Rome.

In essence, becoming a stoic man requires embracing inner strength, resilience, and an unwavering commitment to self-mastery, regardless of external circumstances.

Remember Your Mortality: Embracing Stoic Principles

Memento Mori, a Latin phrase meaning "Remember, one day you will die too," serves as a stark reminder of life's fleeting nature. As a stoic, how can you maintain inner composure and exert control over yourself amidst this reality? It begins with setting a purpose.

Find a goal that challenges you and serves as a test of your character. Whether it's hitting the gym to train your body, enduring discomfort with indifference to pain and pleasure, or developing new skills through consistent practice, use your limited time wisely. Invest your energy in decoding people, mastering new abilities, or shaping your ultimate self.

In your interactions, strive for brevity. Speak only when necessary, and choose your words wisely. Avoid excessive laughter, as indulging in it excessively can detract from your seriousness and focus.

When faced with insults or betrayal, respond with amusement rather than anger. Use humor as a tool to maintain your inner strength and redefine your reality, rather than allowing others to disturb your peace of mind.

Remember, your silence holds power. Use your words sparingly but effectively, as demonstrated by the stoic figure Cato, who wielded his speech with precision and purpose. Like Cato, be prepared to take action when necessary, even if it means facing challenges head-on or making difficult decisions to uphold your principles.

Coping with Infidelity: Embracing Stoicism Amidst Pain

Surviving infidelity can be incredibly challenging, primarily because many individuals succumb to the trap of denial. While it may seem easier to bury one's head in the sand and pretend that everything is fine, denying reality only leads to further physical, mental, and emotional exhaustion. Choosing to ignore the truth will eventually lead to destruction.

However, what many fail to realize is that there are various forms of denial, each equally harmful. I learned this firsthand and hope to spare others from the same ordeal.

Mastering Stoicism During Crisis

Your initial reaction to a crisis sets the tone for how effectively you'll navigate through it. Responding negatively can exacerbate the situation, making it harder to resolve. However, by responding calmly and rationally, you can emerge from any crisis unscathed.

When faced with a crisis, you essentially have two choices: panic and uncertainty, or approach the problem with reason and composure. Opting for the latter allows you to prevent further damage, alleviate suffering, minimize harm, and ultimately bring the crisis to a swift resolution.

If you want to deal with crises well, here are some tips on how to keep a calm and stoic front, no matter what happens.

Always Be Prepared

To tackle crises effectively, it's crucial to maintain a clear head from the start. This requires being reliable and consistent, ready for any impending crisis. Develop an emergency plan to guide you through challenging situations, ensuring you can act swiftly without losing your composure.

However, it's essential to distinguish between "being prepared" and "expecting the worst." While preparation involves optimism and confidence in achieving the best outcome, expecting the worst fosters a mindset of pessimism, anticipating failure regardless of effort.

Stay Vigilant

Many individuals fall into financial ruin because they're caught off guard by crises sneaking up on them. To avoid being blindsided, remain vigilant and observant of your surroundings. By staying attuned to your environment, you'll be better equipped to anticipate and respond to crises before they escalate.

Exercise Caution in Decision-Making

Bad decisions and impulsive behaviors often lead to crises. To mitigate the risk of emergencies, approach decision-making with caution. Take the time to thoroughly assess all facets of a problem, considering various outcomes to determine the best course of action.

If you struggle with impulsive decisions, it may be necessary to delve deeper into your subconscious. Subliminal videos offer a powerful tool for reprogramming your subconscious mind, influencing your thoughts and actions positively. By instilling a sense of calm and focus in your subconscious, you can make more rational decisions and navigate crises with greater resilience.

CONCLUSION

Stoicism, a Hellenistic philosophy, was founded by Zeno of Citium in Athens around the third century BC. Although its roots go back centuries, it gained prominence through practitioners like Epictetus, Seneca, and Marcus Aurelius. Central to Stoic philosophy is the belief that true happiness comes from virtue, particularly wisdom, and that judgment should be based on actions rather than mere words. It emphasizes our control over ourselves and our responses, rather than relying on external events.

Stoicism teaches several important lessons. It reminds us of life's unpredictability and the fleeting nature of our existence. It encourages bravery, good health, and self-control, while highlighting that our discontent often stems from impulsive reactions rather than logical thinking. Unlike some other philosophical schools, Stoicism isn't about complex theories but practical ways to overcome destructive emotions and take meaningful action. It's focused on doing rather than endless debate.

Stoicism has been embraced by people from various walks of life, including kings, presidents, artists, writers, and entrepreneurs. Figures like Frederick the Great and Montaigne found comfort in Stoic teachings during difficult times. Even historical figures like George Washington and Thomas Jefferson were inspired by Stoicism, incorporating its principles into their lives.

Economist Adam Smith's theories on capitalism were also influenced by Stoicism, which he studied extensively. Despite being Roman emperors, Stoics like Marcus Aurelius weren't grumpy or sad; instead, they sought to embody virtue and wisdom in their actions. Stoic philosophy is more akin to a practical guide for life, similar to a yoga class or pre-game warm-up, focusing on cultivating the right mindset for a philosophical life.

Made in United States
Orlando, FL
25 September 2024

51975842R00104